D1626529

"Colin Smith blends the consolations of Scripture with a pastor's heart, watered by tears he has shed for friends walking through deep grief and loss. He does not offer pat answers for questions and mysteries that none but God can fully fathom, but helps sufferers find hope and a route through their pain, carried by His sustaining love and faithfulness."

NANCY DEMOSS WOLGEMUTH
Author; host/teacher of *Revive Our Hearts*

"It is an unusual author and pastor who would dare to take on preaching from the book of Lamentations, but that is what Colin Smith has done in his beautiful work entitled For All Who Grieve. Colin has shown great compassion and sensitivity as he joined together the stories of grief and hurt of five of the families at The Orchard Evangelical Free Church in Illinois, where he has served now for some twenty years, with the teaching of Scripture. In doing so, he has left a great model for his fellow clergymen to follow and for Bible study and Care groups as they too reach out to a huge number of hurting men and women. I highly recommend this book for the body of Christ. It is time we taught God's people how to mourn and how to share tears and conversation with each other towards the healing of the whole body of Christ."

WALTER C. KAISER, JR.
President Emeritus, Gordon-Conwell Theological Seminary, Hamilton, MA

"I'm pretty picky about books I recommend to grieving people. They need to be real about the deep pain of loss, but just as real regarding the healing God intends to do by His Spirit through His Word. And this book excels in both. Readers will find in these pages companionship, understanding, godly wisdom, and hope that it does not have to hurt forever as much as it does today."

NANCY GUTHRIE
Author of *What Grieving People Wish You Knew about What Really Helps (and What Really Hurts)*

"For all those who grieve: Discover how tears are released and seen by God, how loved ones are valued, how guilt meets grace, and how laments turn to confessions of God's comfort. See how grief increases hope and how healing is achieved and maintained by the Counselor who knows all when we do not. Can we who grieve release our claim that no one understands? Proof that we can is found in this book and, most of all, in the One this book shepherds us to see. Colin Smith, with the astute pastoral care for which he is known, offers salient insight concerning the most tender areas of the sorrowing heart; I know because of how my grieving heart has profited by his wisdom."

LIANNA DAVIS
Author of *Made for a Different Land* and *Keeping the Faith*

"Grieving people need comfort from friends and hope from the Bible. Through his pastoral ministry experience and helpful examination of Lamentations, Pastor Colin Smith provides both. This book combines moving stories of real people as they navigated the brokenness of life and the gut-level honesty of biblical lament. It is theological and personal—a rare treasure. If you're hurting or helping someone battling sorrow, For All Who Grieve *is a gift*."

MARK VROEGOP
Lead Pastor at College Park Church, Indianapolis, and author of *Dark Clouds, Deep Mercy*

"Colin Smith has given a gift to parents who have lost children. This book includes rich narratives from couples who have lost children that will help grieving parents feel understood and those who have not lost children to better understand the trauma and grief of such a loss. The book ties together the narratives with rich and honest biblical theology from the book of Lamentations. Smith gives practical, biblical instruction on how to grieve in a manner that is healthy, healing, and godly."

CAMERON COLE
Author of *Therefore I Have Hope*, chairman of Rooted, and Director of Children, Youth and Family at the Cathedral Church of the Advent in Birmingham, AL

FOR ALL WHO GRIEVE

Navigating the Valley of Sorrow and Loss

COLIN S. SMITH

FOR ALL
WHO
GRIEVE

10 Publishing
a division of 10ofthose.com

British Library Cataloguing in Publication Data
A record for this book is available from the British Library

ISBN: 978-1-913278-28-1
Design and typeset by Diane Warnes
Printed in Denmark by Nørhaven & Specialtrykkeriet Arco

10Publishing, a division of 10ofthose.com
Unit C, Tomlinson Road, Leyland, PR25 2DY, England
Email: info@10ofthose.com
Website: www.10ofthose.com

1 3 5 7 10 8 6 4 2

To Greg, Pam, and Lindsey

Lyle and Sue

Wayne and Joyce

Ken, Leslie, and Amy

Stace and Kathy

Betty and Kristen

Your faith and courage in the face of sorrow and loss glorify God and bring strength to all who know you.

CONTENTS

PREFACE

I was out of town on a study break when I picked up a voicemail with the terrible news. A couple in our church had lost their son in a tragic accident.

Over the days that followed, it was my privilege to walk with Greg and Pam in their sorrow. One evening, when my wife, Karen, and I were visiting in their home, I made a rather tentative suggestion. "I don't know if this would be of any interest to you," I said, "but there are other couples in our church who have endured the loss of a child. If you think it would be helpful, Karen and I would be glad to see if we could gather a small group."

I remember how hesitant I felt. "No pressure," I said. "It's just an idea. Perhaps you'd like to think about it over the weekend." The response took me by surprise. "I don't need the weekend to think about *that*," Pam said. "That's something I'd *absolutely* want to do." When Greg agreed, we began to talk about people who might be invited. It was the last Friday in November, and we were talking about getting a group together the following Wednesday, and then meeting each week until Christmas.

Arriving home that evening, I was sure that the group would be helpful but was apprehensive about making the calls. Would anyone be free to come at such short notice? For that matter, would anyone *want* to come, especially so near to Christmas?

One of my fears in extending the invitation was that I might cause further grief, especially for the friends whose loss was many years ago. I was open and candid about this when making the invitation.

"I hesitated before inviting you to join this group," I said to Leslie, whose son Kenny had died 18 years previously. "I don't want you to feel under any pressure, and I wouldn't want this to set you back." I now feel rather foolish about having said that. None of the people I called were being reminded of their loss by my invitation. Their loss is always with them.

To my surprise, everyone we invited wanted to come. Some rearranged their calendars. And five days after making the calls, they were all seated in our front room.

On that first night, each member of the group told their story. Our hearts were quickly bonded together as one reached out to another across the room with love and understanding. It soon became clear that God had brought us together and that He was at work among us in a very special way.

In the weeks that followed, we structured our conversations around the book of Lamentations. I had begun studying this often neglected part of the Bible with a view to preaching it the following year. Its main themes of tears, talk, guilt, grievance, hope, and healing opened up the areas in which we most needed help.

God has given us an entire book of the Bible that shows us how to navigate the valley of grief, sorrow, and loss. Yet in nearly 40 years as a pastor, I had never preached through this book. *Why not?* I had begun to wonder, especially since Lamentations speaks to a painful reality that sooner or later every person will experience.

Our weeks in that small group deepened my understanding of the journey through grief and my conviction that Lamentations is God's gift for those who grieve. Some months later, I preached a short series of sermons on Lamentations at our church. Rarely in my years as a pastor have I seen the Scriptures affect so many people as deeply as I did during these weeks. People connected with the book of Lamentations as they heard its message of pain, sorrow, comfort, and hope. Every week several people asked if I would consider writing this up as a book.

I pondered this for some time and then asked the members of our group if they would like to share what we had experienced together. Everyone agreed. Some of their stories and many of their insights are related in this book. To each of these remarkable people, I extend my heartfelt gratitude.

My prayer for you as you read this book is first that you will gain a better understanding of what it means to grieve and to hope. Christians grieve and hope *at the same time*. We hope while we grieve and we grieve while we hope. People sometimes say, "I don't think I ever grieved properly." If that is your experience, Lamentations, together with the stories in this book, will show you what it looks like to grieve and how to do so with hope.

I also hope you will consider gathering a small group to talk about grief using this book as a basis for discussion. The model our group followed was simple. On the first night, each person in the group shared their story. Then on the evenings that followed, we reflected on the main themes of Lamentations that are taken up in the six chapters of this book. This pattern is easy to follow, and you will find that the questions for reflection and discussion at the end of each chapter will guide your conversations.

Most of all, I hope and pray that when you walk the painful path of sorrow, you will meet with Jesus Christ. The Savior knows what it is to walk sorrow's path, and He is well acquainted with grief. When you pass through the valley of sorrow and loss, you are in a place where Christ can be found. And any path on which you come closer to Him will be blessed, even if it is a path you would never have chosen to walk.

TEARS

TEARS

Lyle and Sue's Story

Lyle and Sue enjoyed having their son home for Christmas, and they were looking forward to what the New Year would bring as John opened a new chapter of his life.

John had enlisted in the army where he served as a combat engineer. After training, he was deployed in Korea and having completed his service, he had returned home to pursue a degree at Harper College in Palatine, Illinois.

Sue recalls John assembling some drawers and shelves she had bought for his room. "When he was done, he went out with his friends. But before he left, he came up behind me, grabbed me round the shoulders, and said, 'I love you Mom.'"

"Well ditto, John. I love you too," Sue said. She didn't know it at the time, but this was her last sweet memory of her son.

The following day was much like any other until late in the afternoon. Sue had been substitute teaching, and when she returned home she noticed a car parked in the road, which was unusual on a dead-end street.

"When I got into the house, I heard a frantic pounding on the door," she said. "I looked through a window and saw a man peering in at me."

"Open up," he said, "I need to talk to you!"

When Sue opened the door, the man identified himself as a police officer.

"Your son has been involved in an accident," he said. "You need to get to the hospital."

"Well, is my son okay?" Sue asked.

"Ma'am, you just need to get to the hospital," the officer replied.

Sue tried to call her husband, Lyle, but she couldn't get hold of him at the school where he was teaching. So, she went across to her neighbor's house.

"John has been in an accident and I need to get to the hospital right away," Sue said. "Please look out for Lyle and tell him where I am."

The neighbor could see that Sue was shaking as she spoke. "You can't drive," she said. "I won't let you drive! Get in the car and I'll take you." Sue remembers arriving at the hospital, but she has very little memory of what happened after that.

Lyle had been supervising an after-school club that afternoon, and he arrived home later than usual. "When I drove into our street, a neighbor flagged me down and told me that John had been in an accident and that I needed to go to the hospital," Lyle said.

When he arrived, a chaplain broke the news that he and Sue had dreaded. Their son was dead.

John had been riding with friends as they made their way toward Harper College for a class. Another student driving in the opposite direction had hit the curb, lost control of his truck, and swerved into the path of the car in which John was traveling. It was a head-on collision, and the three students in the car lost their lives.

———————

Sue has very little memory of the two weeks that followed the accident. She calls this "holy amnesia," and regards these gaps in her memory as a gift from God. "I went around in a stupor," she said, "and all I know of these days is what other people have told me."

Sue was in shock. She kept repeating the same questions over and over again: "Where am I? Why am I here? Did something happen?" In these early days, she would wake up in the night and ask Lyle, "Is there something wrong?"

"Oh, yes," Lyle would reply, "something is *very* wrong."

"What frightened me most," Lyle said, "was what was happening to her, so I decided that we should see a counselor."

"I fought him every inch of the way on that one," Sue said.

"Why, are we going to see a counselor?" she demanded.

"Because I am worried about you," Lyle replied.

Neither Lyle nor Sue can remember much of what the counselor said, but they both recall what was written on the wall in his office: *The only way out is through.*

"The only way out is through."

They also recall the wise words that the counselor gave to Lyle: "Let her see you grieve." That sentence stayed with both of them, but it wasn't easy for Lyle. "The only times I cried were in the middle of the night," he said. "I would get up and go into John's room, and when I was there alone, I would break down in tears."

"Men and women grieve in different ways," Sue said. "I don't think men feel the need to talk as women do, and they don't like to show their emotions."

Lyle agreed. "If something has impacted me deeply, and I try to verbalize it to someone else, I find it hard to get the words out," he said.

———————————

Two weeks after the accident, the InterVarsity group on the Harper College campus held a memorial service for the three students who had died in the accident. Sue wanted to speak about John's spiritual journey at the service, and she asked Lyle what he thought.

"That's fine if you want to do it," Lyle said. "I'm not saying a word, but I will go up and stand beside you."

The memorial service proved helpful to Sue. "For the first two weeks it was as if I was asleep," she said, "but after the service it seemed as if I woke up again."

> *"At first I couldn't cry, but when I started, I couldn't stop!"*

Waking up meant facing the intense pain from which Sue had been shielded during her days in the twilight. "I was numb during these first two weeks. There was pain there for sure, but I really don't remember feeling very much at all. But when I woke up, the pain was awful," she said. "At first I couldn't cry, but when I started, I couldn't stop!"

THE STORY BEHIND LAMENTATIONS

The grieving people in Lamentations couldn't stop crying either. They had endured five disasters, one on top of the other.

First, enemies laid siege to their city: "In the ninth year of his reign... Nebuchadnezzar king of Babylon came with all his army against Jerusalem, and laid siege to it" (Jeremiah 52:4).

Second, with no supplies entering the city, food soon became scarce, and the struggle for survival became increasingly desperate: "All her people groan as they search for bread" (Lamentations 1:11).

Starving people can only hold out for a limited time. And so, third, the city of Jerusalem fell: "Her people fell into the hand of the foe" (Lamentations 1:7).

Fourth, when the walls of Jerusalem were breached, the invading army occupied the city and God's people found themselves under the heel of a brutal oppressor: "Her foes have become the head" (Lamentations 1:5).

And fifth, the temple where God's presence had come down was completely destroyed: "The holy stones lie scattered at the head of every street" (Lamentations 4:1).

WHERE WAS GOD IN ALL OF THIS?

Lamentations is a lament—a long, loud, and agonized cry—ascending to God from people who endured unspeakable loss. Many of these people had lost children. The youngest would have been the first to die of starvation during the siege of the city. And when the city fell, those who had older children endured the pain of seeing their sons and daughters marched off into exile, knowing that they would never see them again: "Her children have gone away, captives before the foe" (Lamentations 1:5).

In addition to the loss of their children, the survivors in Jerusalem had suffered the trauma of horrendous atrocities. Some were abused: "Women are raped in Zion, young women in the towns of Judah" (Lamentations 5:11). Others were enslaved: "Young men are compelled to grind at the mill, and boys stagger under loads of wood" (Lamentations 5:13).

Homes that were once filled with music, love, and laughter were destroyed, and God's people were reduced to scratching a living in the ruins and rubble of their once glorious city: "The joy of our hearts has ceased, our dancing has been turned to mourning" (Lamentations 5:15).

Jeremiah had the unenviable task of being God's mouthpiece at this desperate time. Picture him walking through the rubble of the once great city of God, as the smoke rises from the ashes. The city that once bustled with people now seems like a ghost town. "How lonely sits the city that was full of people," he says. "She weeps bitterly in the night, with tears on her cheeks" (Lamentations 1:1-2).

A RELEASE VALVE FOR YOUR PAIN

Lamentations is a book soaked in tears:

> For these things I weep; my eyes flow with tears; for a comforter is far from me. (Lamentations 1:16)

> My eyes are spent with weeping. (Lamentations 2:11)

> My eyes flow with rivers of tears because of the destruction of the daughter of my people. (Lamentations 3:48)

> My eyes will flow without ceasing, without respite, until the LORD from heaven looks down and sees. (Lamentations 3:49-50)

Notice that these references to tears don't dry up after the first chapter. They continue throughout the book, so don't be surprised if your tears continue too.

Tears are the shuddering of the body at the pain of the soul. They are a gift from God, because they act as a release valve for your pain. So let your tears flow and don't hold them back.

> "Tears are the shuddering of the body at the pain of the soul."

One of the unnerving things about tears is that you never know when they are going to come next. They come at unexpected times. One member of our group reminded us of the hymn that says, "When sorrows like sea billows roll."[1]

"Sorrow comes in waves," she said, "and a new wave can be set off by a sight, a sound, or a smell." She then described a time when a fragrance reminded her of the smell of her son's hair, and another wave of grief came crashing over her. No one could have known the cause of her sudden and unexpected distress.

Another member of our group told us that people often said to her, "I don't know what to say to you because I don't want to make you cry." Her answer was simple, "If you make me cry, you are only taking me to a place where I already live most of the time."

Sometimes the tears just won't come. When Sue told us that she had been in a state of shock and that she couldn't cry for days, other members of the group identified with her experience. One said that she had felt guilty because she wasn't crying. *Why did the tears not come?* she wondered.

The shock of a sudden loss can freeze your senses so that you don't feel what you would expect to feel. Lamentations reflects this experience: "He has left me stunned, faint all the day long" (Lamentations 1:13). A person who is stunned has no feeling, and this numbness is often part of shock, especially in the early days of bereavement.

You can't force tears, but when they come, don't hold them back! God says, "Let tears stream down like a torrent day and night! Give yourself no rest, your eyes no respite!... Pour out your heart like water before the presence of the Lord" (Lamentations 2:18–19).

ARE TEARS A SIGN OF WEAKNESS?

God gave you tear ducts for a reason, and no Christian should ever be ashamed of his or her tears.

The tears in Lamentations were produced by the Spirit of God. This book is Scripture, and "all Scripture is breathed out by

"God gave you tear ducts for a reason."

God" (2 Timothy 3:16). The tears welling up in the eyes of Jeremiah as he walked through the ruins of Jerusalem were more than the effect of his pain. They were the work of the Spirit of God within him. The tears of Lamentations came directly from the throne of God.

But sometimes the feeling persists that tears are a sign of weakness. A woman in our congregation wrote to me expressing what I suspect is the feeling of many:

> I was eager to hear this series on grief because we've gone through loss. I've had two miscarriages and I have only shared this with those close to me. I felt that I had to hold things together and that if I didn't I would not be a faithful Christian. So it was good to hear that it's okay to cry and to know what Scripture says about our tears.

If you feel that tears are a sign of weakness, remember that Jesus wept. The Apostle John records the story of the visit of Jesus to Martha and Mary, the sisters of Lazarus with whom Jesus was especially close. Lazarus had died, and, a few days after the funeral, Jesus arrived in

Bethany where Martha and Mary were grieving the loss of their dearly loved brother.

When Jesus saw Mary weeping, He was deeply moved in His spirit, and when He came to the tomb where Lazarus was buried, "Jesus wept" (John 11:35).

Why did Jesus weep? Certainly not because Jesus had lost hope. Our Lord knew that the day of resurrection had come for Lazarus. In just a few minutes, Christ would raise him from the dead. Jesus told Martha, "Your brother will rise again" (John 11:23).

But notice that Jesus did *not* say, "Your brother will rise again, so don't grieve." Jesus says, "I am the resurrection and the life" (John 11:25), but He still weeps with those who weep (John 11:35).

Never make the mistake of thinking that weeping means you are failing to believe adequately in the resurrection. Jesus had tears rolling down His face over the death of a dearly loved friend. He wept over death even though He knew that for Lazarus resurrection was only moments away!

PEOPLE GRIEVE IN DIFFERENT WAYS

Many years have passed since that awful day when Lyle and Sue's lives were forever changed by the devastating news of the sudden loss of their son. Their loss placed an enormous strain on them and on their marriage, but by the grace of God, they have emerged with a stronger faith and a deeper love.

Like many other couples, Lyle and Sue have different strengths. Lyle is quiet, steady, and rock solid. Sue is intense, insightful, and articulate. God knew what He was doing when He brought them together, and through their sorrow, they have come to a deeper appreciation of each other's strengths.

Looking back, Sue sees the strength and stability that Lyle displayed while she was "asleep." "He made all the calls. He did whatever needed to be done," she said.

In our group we spoke at length about the strain that grief places on a marriage. Lyle and Sue's insight that men and women often grieve in different ways resonated around the room. No one was surprised that Lyle had difficulty with the wise words of the counselor, who told him to let his wife see him grieve. Nor were any of us surprised that Sue had misread her husband's lack of tears and mistakenly assumed that he was not grieving.

Leslie, whose story we will hear in chapter 3, gave us the help and insight we all needed on this point. She and her husband, Ken, also faced difficulties because of their very different ways of handling grief.

"It's true," Leslie said. "Men and women grieve differently and I struggled with this. But I came to see that my husband was the only other person on the planet who loved our son like I did and was a part of him as I was. We were bound together in our grief, and however different our ways of coping, he was one with me in it as no one else could ever be."

THE POWER OF THANKSGIVING

Looking back on the early days of her sorrow, Sue recalls the sense of falling into a dark pit. She felt that she was sinking. How could she get out?

"Part of the journey of healing for me came through thanking God for the smallest gifts in my life," Sue said. "I thanked Him that the sky was blue and that the sun was shining. If a bird was singing, I would thank Him that at least the bird could sing. And every time I gave thanks, it felt as if I was taking a tiny step towards climbing out of that awful pit."

Sue made extensive use of the Scriptures, especially of the Psalms, in her journey through grief. They gave her words when she had none and helped her to pray, asking God for what He had promised. She also formed the helpful habit of putting her name into verses of Scripture as she read them, applying what God had said to her own situation. Reading the first two verses of Psalm 40, she would say:

> Sue waited patiently for the LORD;
> He inclined to Sue and heard her cry.
> He drew Sue up from the pit of destruction,
> out of the miry bog,
> And set Sue's feet upon a rock,
> making her steps secure.

"The Psalms put words to what I was feeling," she said. "They gave me permission to feel these things, and they helped to guide my thoughts and my emotions."

Sue was especially helped by David's prayer, "Put my tears in your bottle. Are they not in your book?" (Psalm 56:8). This marvelous verse reminded her that the tears of believers are

> *"The Psalms put words to what I was feeling."*

precious to God. Not one of them is ever forgotten. Every tear you have ever shed is captured by your heavenly Father, and God wants you to know that all the pain you have ever experienced is completely known to Him. Other people will only see a small part of your sorrow, but none of it is hidden from the Lord.

One day Christ will wipe away all tears from your eyes (Revelation 21:4). That is a staggering promise, and right now, you may wonder if it is even possible. Wiping away all tears is something that only God Himself could do. But He has said that He will do it. Literally, God says He will wipe all tears "out of" your eyes, as if in the resurrection body God would take away not only your tears but also the source of them. Tear ducts will no longer be needed when the springs of sorrow are gone.

That day has not yet come. And until it does there will be tears. But God has given you a Savior who knows what it is to weep. Our Lord was a man of sorrows, and He was well acquainted with grief (Isaiah 53:3). Christ plumbed the depths of sorrow when He suffered on the cross, and no one is more ready or more able to walk with you through the valley of sorrow and loss than Jesus Christ. So don't be afraid to let your tears flow. Christ will dry them in His own time.

QUESTIONS FOR REFLECTION AND DISCUSSION

1. What did you most relate to in Lyle and Sue's story? Why?

2. Why might a Christian feel that they should hold back their tears? What would you say to help them?

3. The Bible tells us that Jesus wept. What's your reaction to that?

4. What does it mean to you to know that none of your grief is hidden from God?

5. Where have you caught glimpses of God's mercy in your journey through grief?

TALK

TALK

Wayne and Joyce's Story

Wayne and Joyce were on vacation in a rental home in Florida with their four daughters aged ten, eight, five, and two. Wayne's parents had joined them, as had Joyce's mother. It was a full house.

Joyce was preparing lunch for the extended family in the kitchen that looked out over a swimming pool in the yard. Wayne was playing a round of golf with his cousins, and the children were in the living room, along with the three grandparents.

As we talked together, Joyce described the moment that is forever fixed in her memory. "I looked up from the sink, and to my horror, saw our youngest daughter, Jill, floating in the pool."

In a moment of blind panic, Joyce rushed into the water and lifted her daughter out. "I shouted to the grandparents to call 911, and tried to do what I could, but she was gone," she said.

To this day, Joyce does not know how her two-year-old got out of the house and into the pool. "As far as I was aware, she was playing in the living room with her sisters and her grandparents. How she got out of the house remains a mystery to me."

Wayne had just finished playing golf when one of his cousins received a call there had been an accident at the rental property and that Wayne should get there as soon as possible. When he arrived at the house, he received the tragic news that Jill had drowned in the swimming pool. She was two years and twenty-four days old.

Night came, but sleep was impossible. Joyce spent the night awake in the living room, listening to the incessant chirping of birds through the early hours of the morning. "I hated that sound," she said. "For years after Jill died, the sound of birds in the morning brought back the feeling of that awful pain."

———————————

Wayne and Joyce returned home as soon as they were able to book the flights. "I felt paralyzed by what had happened," Joyce said. "I didn't want to get out of bed, and went for about a week like that. The thought of getting up and starting a new day was just too much for me. Then one of my friends brought me some flats of flowers for planting in the garden. She knew that I liked flowers and that I wouldn't let them die. It was a really clever thing to do, and it worked. I got up and planted the flowers."

The months that followed were a whirlwind of relentless activity for Wayne and Joyce. Jill died on April 27, and her funeral was in May. "I couldn't cry at the wake," Joyce said, "and I couldn't stand music being played."

Then Wayne's father died in June, and the family was plunged into another journey of grief and loss. "By that time I was crying good," Joyce said. "At first the tears wouldn't come, but when they started, they wouldn't stop."

> "At first the tears wouldn't come, but when they started, they wouldn't stop."

In July, their five-year-old daughter had her tonsils out, a simple enough procedure, but one that brought Joyce great anxiety. "My sense of being able to protect my daughter had been shattered," she said.

A few weeks later, all three of the girls came down with chickenpox, but by August they had recovered and were ready for the start of school. For Joyce this meant that, for the first time, all of her daughters would be at school, a major milestone for any mother.

In September, the pastor of their church invited Joyce to work as his assistant for a few months. She accepted the invitation and found the stimulus of this part-time work to be helpful.

Then in October, Joyce found that she was pregnant! Soon after their loss, Wayne and Joyce had decided that they would like to have another child, and God blessed them with that gift quickly. So the traumatic spring and the relentless summer gave way to the demands of pregnancy in the fall and then to the arrival of a new baby the following year.

More than 40 years have passed since Jill's death, and in all of that time, Wayne and Joyce had rarely spoken about their loss. "You have all these feelings and you never really have the opportunity to discuss your thoughts with someone else," Wayne said. "But the grief group was different. This was in-depth. We weren't just talking about surface things."

Knowing that each family in the group had lost a child helped Wayne and Joyce to tell their story, but it wasn't easy. "On that first evening when we gathered in your home with the others, I thought that Wayne would tell our story and I wouldn't have to," Joyce told me. "So I was rather shocked when you looked at me and asked me to speak. It was so traumatic for me to tell the story that I was shaking for at least an hour afterwards. But it brought a release and a cleansing. I had no idea this would happen, but to sit in that group and say that I had lost a child was freeing for me."

One reason Joyce avoided speaking about Jill was her fear of someone asking how her daughter died. "I could never say that Jill had drowned," she said. "I think that was tied to my sense of guilt over what had happened. So for years, I have said that I have four daughters. It has only been in these last months I have felt able to say that I have five daughters: Four of them are here and one is in heaven."

Looking back on their journey, Wayne and Joyce are grateful for the help and support they received from their pastor. He met them from the plane when they returned from Florida. He visited regularly and typed up cards with personalized prayers that Wayne and Joyce could use. But the pastor said something on their arrival back home that stayed with Joyce and troubled her deeply: "When you receive communion you will be forgiven." What did that mean?

"I carried that with me," Joyce said, "and I felt that I needed forgiveness for what had happened. We never spoke of it again, but what he said weighed on me for years."

Wayne also struggled with a sense of guilt. "My job carried a lot of responsibility, and I rarely had time on my own," he said. "But I would cry in the car on my way home, and often thought that I should have been there in the house rather than out on the golf course."

Both Wayne and Joyce were helped by the group's conversation on guilt (which is the focus of chapter 3 in this book). "It's only recently that I've really grasped the forgiveness that comes through what Jesus did for us on the cross and how we are still going to be with Him in heaven, even though we continue to sin," Joyce said. "That's a really difficult concept to get hold of."

"I can't believe it has taken so long to understand so many things about the Lord," she continued. "We always believed, always went to church, always had religion in our lives. But we never had the deep understanding that getting into the Bible has created. I feel so blessed to finally have this now."

HOW TO GRIEVE PROPERLY

Grief is the painful process of adapting to the loss of something or someone you love. It may be the loss of a spouse or a child. It could be the loss of your health—the physical ability or the mental capacity to pursue something you greatly enjoyed. Or it might be the loss of a role or position.[2]

When a person loses a loved one, we speak of them as being bereaved. The word *reave* means to rob, plunder, or tear away, and when you lose someone you love, this is what you feel. Your loved one has been taken from you, and you are *reaved*, literally torn in two.

> *"Grief builds in the soul like steam in a boiler, and the pressure of grief that is not expressed can break your heart."*

Grief builds in the soul like steam in a boiler, and the pressure of grief that is not expressed can break your heart. So we must find ways to release the pressure. God has provided for this first through the gift of tears and then through the gift of talk.

Lamentations puts grief into words. It is a sustained outpouring of sorrow in which the painful details of all that happened to God's people, and all that they lost, are repeated over and over again. The five chapters of Lamentations often seem to go around in circles. Grief is like that. It is not linear. Grieving people know what it is to cover the same ground again and again.

Imagine a priceless vase or ornament that falls to the floor and is smashed. The woman who loved it kneels down and picks up the pieces. She looks at each one in detail, holding up even the smallest piece to the light and turning it around as if to remember where it once belonged. That's what grief is like.

A grieving person will often want to talk about the smallest detail of their loss. They may focus a great deal of attention on what seems like an inconsequential aspect of their story, and you may wonder why this piece is so important to them. It is important because it was part of something dearly loved. It had its place in what was cherished and now has been lost.

God has given us an entire book of the Bible in which sorrow is put into words and the grief of what was lost is expressed over and over again. This tells us something very important about how to grieve: We must give sorrow words. Telling your story will be part of God's provision for healing your soul.

Telling your story of sorrow and loss will not be easy, especially if your experience was traumatic. Joyce's experience of shaking for an hour after she told her story to our group shows how difficult it can be, especially if your story has been tightly guarded over a long period of time. But Wayne and Joyce found that telling their story brought "a release and a cleansing." Great help will come to you through sharing your story with others who are in a position to understand.

Those who have suffered the most traumatic experiences will often find it most difficult to share what they have seen and endured. If you have survived a horrific experience, you should choose whom you will share this with carefully. Consider whether they can relate to what you suffered and whether they are able to bear the weight of what you might share

> *"The more difficult a story is to tell, the more important it is that it should be told."*

with them. But, as a general rule, the more difficult a story is to tell, the more important it is that it should be told. This is where groups that bring people with shared experiences together can be especially helpful.

TRAUMA, MEMORY, AND FLASHBACKS

Lamentations includes some gruesome scenes from the days of the siege, and since the book was written after the city had fallen, we would call these flashbacks. Today, we are very aware of the delayed or accumulated impact on the mind and heart of traumatic events that stay in our minds and replay themselves over and over again. Anyone who has experienced trauma or suffered violence knows what it is to say, "my soul continually remembers it" (Lamentations 3:20). What you endured comes back to you when you are in the car, in the shower, and, most of all, when you are in bed at night. Whenever your mind is at rest, the memory of what you endured is close at hand.

One member of our group who endured the sudden and tragic loss of his son said, "I think that anyone who experiences a traumatic event will have flashbacks in one form or another. At first it was nearly all day long. As time passes it is becoming less frequent, but it sneaks up on me in many ways. Sometimes I see him lying there and I can shift my thoughts to something else. Other times I think through the entire weekend when he died, and before I know it, there he is. Or if I think about events afterward, I find myself backing into it. It is a battle each day."

There are no easy answers to the pain and persistence of these flashbacks. It is surely significant, however, that when God's people endured the horrors of seeing their children die, and then faced the trauma of violence, torture, rape, and forced labor, they put what they had seen into words.

Lamentations is not for the fainthearted. Disturbing scenes are recorded in graphic detail (Lamentations 2:19–21; 4:10). Why? Because these things happened, and they remained in the minds and hearts of those who saw them.

God caused every excruciating detail of what they had experienced to be written down. Nothing was glossed over. The story of what God's people suffered was told with no details spared and nothing held back. Going through the story is always painful, but it will help Healing comes when you face the darkest corners of your pain, trauma, grief, and loss and bring it out into the light of God's healing presence in the company of others who love you.

KEEPING MEMORIES ALIVE

G. K. Chesterton (1874–1936) experienced loss early in life when his sister, Beatrice, died at the age of eight. In a style that was not unusual at the time, Chesterton's father responded to the loss by turning Beatrice's picture to face the wall, getting rid of all her possessions, and forbidding anyone to mention her name.[3]

Nothing could be further from the pattern God has given us in Lamentations, where He tells us how to grieve. Silence is not the answer; fellowship is. And that happens when grieving people speak, and when others who love them listen.

A pastor by the name of Donald Howard wrote a helpful booklet in which he reflects on what he learned from his experience of losing his wife, who died of cancer in her forties.

"Let the bereaved speak," he says, but then he points out that too often, the opposite happens. A widow is with friends and one of them remembers a funny story about her husband. Out of consideration for the widow, he holds the story back and steers the conversation in another direction. "Had he told the story," Howard comments, "she probably would have laughed; perhaps there might have been a tear or two in her eyes, but *she would have thought it wonderful that he was still remembered*." Then Howard makes this striking remark: "Part of the congregation's task as time goes by is to help keep the memory of loved ones alive."[4]

> "Part of the congregation's task as time goes by is to help keep the memory of loved ones alive."

Don't be afraid to speak about someone who has died to a person who loves them. One member of our group said that, for a bereaved person, it is always a gift to bring up their loved one's name. If you have good memories of a person who has died, the one who grieves his or her loss will want to hear them, and they will be glad that the one they love is still remembered.

Those who sorrow often wonder, *Does anyone else remember? Does anyone else share my sense of loss?* Speaking about someone who has died answers these questions, and helps a grieving person by keeping the memory of their loved one alive.

GOD'S CHILDREN SHOULD NEVER GRIEVE ALONE

God calls us to "weep with those who weep" (Romans 12.15). This is not a suggestion but a command in which God makes it clear that grieving is something He wants us to do with others. While there are depths of sorrow that only the bereaved person can know, it is never the will of God that any of His children should grieve alone. Eugene Peterson says:

> One of the strategies of pastoral work is to enter private grief and make a shared event of it. The biblical way to deal with suffering is to transform what is individual into something corporate.

> Pastoral work cannot adequately function if it is limited to private comfort and individual consolation. The neighbors must be brought into the room, the congregation must gather so that the sufferers come to realize that the pain they cannot resign themselves to is understood by others.[5]

Two things must happen if Christians are to weep with those who weep. First, there must be brothers and sisters in Christ who are ready to sit with those who grieve and identify with their sorrow. And second, those who grieve must be open to these brothers and sisters and allow them into their sorrow.

Thankfully, our culture is much more in touch with the importance of speaking about pain and loss than was often the case when G. K. Chesterton was young. But it is not uncommon for grieving Christians to put on a brave face and to insist that any tears will be shed in private where no one will see them.

In recent years, it has become popular to redesignate a funeral service as a "celebration of life." And it is not unusual for a bereaved person to insist that it should be an upbeat occasion. But if even a funeral is no longer a place to grieve, what place is left for the expression of sorrow and loss? This privatizing of grief is very different from the pattern God gives us in Lamentations where the sorrows of God's people are shared and their stories of loss are heard.

> *"God calls your brothers and sisters to weep with you, but that can only happen if you will allow others to walk with you in your sorrow."*

God calls your brothers and sisters to weep with you, but that can only happen if you will allow others to walk with you in your sorrow. The body of Christ is part of God's provision for you, so allow others into your grief and loss.

TALKING ABOUT YOUR LOVED ONE

Wise people choose who they share their deepest thoughts with carefully. Some are better able to listen than others. Some have deeper compassion than others. Those who have walked the valley of sorrow will relate to your loss in a deeper way than others who have yet to pass through it.

So choose whom you talk with carefully, and as you do, remember that there is One who, more than any other, knows what it is to walk sorrow's path. He calls out to you from the book of Lamentations and says, "Look and see if there is any sorrow like my sorrow" (Lamentations 1:12). You have a Savior with whom you can talk. He is full of compassion, and He is always ready to listen to you.

So talk to God about your loss, and remember when you do that He knows you completely. David said to God, "You have kept count of my tossings" (Psalm 56:8). God sees every time you turn in your bed on a sleepless night. He already knows your darkest thoughts and your deepest fears, so when you speak to Him there is nothing you ever need to hide.

A great gulf is fixed between this world and the next, and you cannot talk to your loved one who has died. But you can talk *about* your loved one to the Savior. You can tell the Lord how much you miss him. You can tell the Lord how much you love her. And if your loved one was in Christ, you can do this knowing that he or she is very close to the One with whom you are speaking.

QUESTIONS FOR REFLECTION
AND DISCUSSION

1. What did you relate to in Wayne and Joyce's story?

2. Who are the people in your life that you can talk to about your grief?

3. Can you think of a time when you intentionally decided not to share your grief? What happened?

4. God calls us to "weep with those who weep." Who could you be intentional about weeping with? What might that look like?

5. What sounds, smells, or sights tend to bring back the memory of your loss? Why?

GUILT

GUILT

Ken and Leslie's Story

Ken got into his car and headed out to Camp Timber-lee, the camp where he was widely appreciated as the "king of gifts in kind." Ken has a knack for motivating people to volunteer time, talent, goods, and services for a good cause. For many years, he had deployed that gift for the benefit of the camp. Ken's 13-year-old son, Kenny, was with him, along with a friend to whom Kenny wanted to show the camp while his dad was immersed in meetings.

The day started brightly enough, but as it wore on, Kenny began to feel sick. By the time his dad was ready to return, he was exhausted. On the journey home, he laid down in the back of the car, and when they arrived, Kenny went to bed.

Leslie had completed her shift as a nurse, and she was working on her computer when her husband and son arrived home.

"How was your day?" she asked.

"It went fine," Ken answered, "but Kenny isn't feeling too good. He's gone upstairs."

"Poor kid," Leslie replied, "I'll go and check on him."

When Leslie went upstairs, she found Kenny sprawled out, face down on the bed. When she shook him, he was burning hot, and when she tried to rouse him, he barely responded. "Ken, something is *very* wrong," Leslie shouted. "We've got to get Kenny to the hospital."

Doctors at the local hospital quickly diagnosed that Kenny had gone into septic shock, and they arranged for him to be flown to Lutheran General Hospital, where he was rushed into intensive care. Ken and Leslie made the hour-long journey by car, not knowing whether their son would be dead or alive when they arrived.

Kenny survived that first battle. He woke up the next morning not really knowing what had happened to him, and apologized to his dad as if he had done something wrong. Shortly thereafter, Kenny was diagnosed with leukemia, and a course of chemotherapy was prescribed. The doctors said his chances of recovery were fifty-fifty.

Knowing that his son was facing a serious condition, Ken had an honest heart-to-heart with Kenny. "This isn't monkey business, son. This is pretty serious," he said. "You could die from this. We don't know which way this is going. Anything could happen. It's in God's hands."

Kenny had a clear answer: "Dad, you know I am a Christian." He knew where he was going if the chemotherapy failed.

In the weeks that followed, Ken and Leslie alternated shifts at the hospital so that one of them was with Kenny at any given time. They spent Thanksgiving, Christmas, and New Year's Eve at Kenny's bedside.

"There were some very lonely nights and days when I felt far from God," Leslie said. "I didn't feel that I could pray, and when I did, I felt that no one was listening. I was lonely and afraid. And Ken and I were apart during this time, so we had little opportunity to talk about what was happening."

The first round of chemo went smoothly enough, but in the second round, Kenny started losing his hair. He kept a good sense of humor through all of this, and there were times when it seemed that he might pull through. But as the new year began, Kenny took a turn for the worse, and a week later, he became very sick.

Leslie recalls her alarm as she arrived at the hospital that day. "He was pale, and to my nurse's eye, he didn't look right. I grabbed a stethoscope and listened to his heart. It sounded strangely irregular. Then I felt for a pulse, but could not find one. Something was very wrong."

Leslie called for help. A nurse arrived and a doctor ordered an EKG. While they were waiting for the technician to arrive, Kenny had a seizure. "Boy that was weird," he said after it subsided. "You know when a train goes past and you hear the 'whoosh' of the cars? That's what just happened to me!"

Then, in a moment when he was alone with his mom in the room, Kenny said, "Mom, I love you."

"That's very precious to me," Leslie said. "It was the last 'I love you' I heard from him, and these were some of Kenny's last words."

A few minutes later Kenny had what appeared to be a massive seizure. Leslie ran to get help. A "Code Blue" was called, followed by relentless activity as many staff arrived. Kenny was indeed having a seizure, and on top of that, he was in cardiac arrest.

> *"I remember feeling as if I was falling into a dark pit. I kept falling, falling, falling, but I never hit the bottom."*

Feeling unable to watch the doctors resuscitate her son, Leslie stood in a small nook close to Kenny's room. "I remember feeling as if I was falling into a dark pit. I kept falling, falling, falling, but I never hit the bottom. I felt as if there was a net beneath me as I fell. Someone was holding me under both of my arms. It was a feeling of support that is hard to describe. I believe that there were many who were praying for us that night and that the support I felt was Christ holding me up and keeping me from hitting the bottom of the pit."

Leslie was stunned when, about half an hour later, a doctor came out and told her, "I stopped CPR and was coming to tell you that Kenny had died, when his heart started beating again!"

Kenny was taken back to the intensive care unit, where he remained in a coma for another five days. But Leslie was again alone at the hospital when she received the news that her son's heart had been severely damaged and that his brain was dead. "What was I supposed to do with this information? Kenny was going to die and I was losing a piece of myself. I felt hopeless."

Over those five days, family and friends had time to say goodbye to Kenny. "It was the hardest time of my life," Leslie said. "We turned off the machines that were sustaining Kenny's life and allowed him to slip away. I remember holding out my arms symbolically as if to say, 'Here you go God, you can have him back.' But I don't think I really meant it. As Kenny died, it seemed as if my heart was being pulled out of my chest. I felt as if I was being ripped in two, and I thought I was going to die there and then."

Seven-and-a-half weeks had passed since the bright November morning when Kenny had gone to enjoy a day at the camp with his dad. These weeks had been exhausting, and now Ken and Leslie faced a long journey through the valley of grief and loss.

Leslie recalls the silence as she and Ken drove home from the hospital with their two daughters. "We sat in numbness staring out of the windows as we drove back home. I remember seeing people in other cars laughing and having a good time. I had

> *"When the sun rose the following morning, Leslie wondered how the world could go on spinning when her world had completely stopped."*

just lost my only son, and these people were smiling. How dare they!" When the sun rose the following morning, Leslie wondered how the world could go on spinning when her world had completely stopped.

———

"It hit Leslie more immediately than it hit me," Ken said as we talked about how the trauma had affected him. "She was there when everything went down. I think for dads it may take a year or two before the finality really sinks in. Leslie took extended time off work after Kenny died. With all that she had been through, she didn't want to be around hospitals for a while. But I function best when I am working."

"I have my moments when I have to walk away and cry," Ken continued. "I've got horseshoe pits in the backyard. Kenny and his buddies would throw horseshoes, and one of them got lost in the bushes. We never found it. But years later, I was clearing out the hedge and there it was, the lost horseshoe. That set me off. The last person to touch that horseshoe was Kenny."

"Time heals a little bit, but the loss is always there. I lost my dad 30 years ago, when he was 60. That was in the normal course of life, but burying your son is against the course of nature."

Looking back over the 18 years that had passed since Kenny's death, Ken was able to identify specific ways in which the direction of other people's lives had been changed through the loss that he and his family have suffered. "God's grace is tremendously powerful," he said. "I can't imagine getting through this without His grace."

"For 18 years I have been troubled by regret over what else I might have done."

After the second group meeting in our home, Leslie realized that she was still struggling with guilt over the death of her son. "For 18 years I have been troubled by regret over what else I might have done when Kenny had his cardiac arrest," she said. "I called for help and then left the room while the doctors attended to him. Would there have been a different outcome if I had taken direct action myself?"

Leslie had rarely spoken about these feelings of guilt. When she did, she had been told that she was dealing with "false guilt" and that she needed to put it behind her. But the moments that followed Kenny's seizure continued to haunt her, and her sense of guilt remained.

Grief invariably has its "what ifs" and its "if onlys:" "If only I had called the doctor sooner. If only I had visited my loved one when I could. If only we had not planned that trip. If only we had not argued as we did."

When you lose someone you love, you may find that things you said or did years ago come back to mind, even though they had long been forgotten. Harsh words you said and foolish things you did rise up and hammer on your conscience, bringing a renewed sense of guilt.

Sometimes these issues relate directly to the death of a loved one. A loyal spouse, who has kept watch by a bedside for days, steps out of the room for a few hours, and cannot forgive him or herself for not being there at the end. Then, on top of all the "what ifs" and the "if onlys," there is the awful feeling of unfinished business, especially if your loss was sudden or unexpected and you never had the chance to say goodbye.

BOOKENDS ON THE SPECTRUM OF GUILT

Grief usually comes with guilt attached, and honest conversation about guilt was an important part of our group's interaction. Everyone had regret over something they did or failed to do in relation to the loss of their loved one.

I opened our conversation by pointing out that the Bible has not one, but two books that deal directly with the themes of grief, sorrow, and loss. One of these is Lamentations, the other is the book of Job, and there are important differences between them.

Guilt is written all over Lamentations, but it plays no part whatsoever in the story of Job. God describes Job as "a blameless and upright man, who fears God and turns away from evil" (Job 1:8).

Job's friends did not believe this. They were convinced that God brings good to the righteous and trouble to the wicked. When they saw Job suffer, they concluded that God must be punishing him for some secret sin in his life. Job's best course of action, they counseled, would be to tell the truth and make an open confession of whatever sin he had kept hidden. But Job refused to accept that his suffering was a result of personal sin. "I am in the right," he insisted, "I am blameless" (Job 9:15, 20, 21).

At the end of the story, God stood with Job and rebuked his friends: "My anger burns against you... for you have not spoken of me what is right, as my servant Job has" (Job 42:7).

Job's friends were not alone in their assumption that all suffering can be traced back to some personal sin. The disciples of Jesus fell into the same error when, on meeting a blind man, they asked, "Rabbi, who sinned, this man or his parents, that he was born blind?" (John 9:2).

Our Lord's reply could not have been clearer; "It was not that this man sinned, or his parents, but that the works of God might be displayed in him" (John 9:3).

Lamentations might lead you to conclude that all suffering is a direct result of personal sin. But that is not the case, as the book of Job and the teaching of Jesus make abundantly clear. Some suffering is allowed by God so that His mighty work might be displayed in the life of the person who suffers, and this is modeled for us in the Old Testament by Job and in the New Testament by the blind man who was healed by Jesus.

But alongside the book of Job where guilt plays no part, God has given us the book of Lamentations that is saturated with guilt. Here we find suffering people who know that what they have endured is directly related to their own sin. While Job repeatedly protests his innocence, these people repeatedly confess their guilt:

"The LORD is in the right, for I have rebelled against his word" (Lamentations 1:18).

"Look, O LORD, for I am in distress; my stomach churns; my heart is wrung within me, *because I have been very rebellious.*" (1:20, italics added)

"Deal with them as you have dealt with me *because of all my transgressions.*" (1:22, italics added)

"*We have transgressed and rebelled,* and you have not forgiven." (3:42, italics added)

> This was for the sins of her prophets and the iniquities of her priests. (4:13)

> The punishment *of your iniquity*, O daughter of Zion, is accomplished. (4:22, italics added).

These confessions of guilt from God's beleaguered people run throughout the book of Lamentations, bringing to mind the words of the thief on the cross, who said to his colleague, "We are receiving the due reward of our deeds" (Luke 23:41).

In Lamentations, God's people suffered as a direct result of their own sin. But Job makes it clear that suffering also comes to blameless and upright people.

Job and Lamentations stand as the bookends on the spectrum of guilt in grief and loss. Most people experience something in-between. We believe that God is for us, but we struggle with our "what ifs" and our "if onlys" and wonder if different choices might have led to a different outcome for the person we love.

And sometimes there is the sneaking suspicion that God has been catching up with you, and that if you had been more faithful to Him, He might not have taken the person you love.

Grief usually comes with some guilt attached. If the only book in the Bible that dealt with loss was one in which the sufferer was able to say "I am blameless," we would lack something that we desperately need: a model of how to confess what lies on your conscience. So thank God for Lamentations.

DEALING WITH TRUE AND FALSE GUILT

If you have something on your conscience, don't ignore it in the hope that it will go away, and don't let people persuade you that it doesn't matter. Your conscience is a gift from God, and its voice must be heard.

There may be times when your conscience accuses you falsely, but even then, the answer is not to ignore your conscience. People may tell you to "give yourself a break" or to "lighten up"

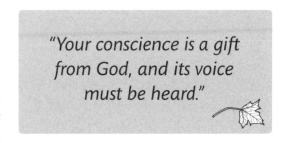

"Your conscience is a gift from God, and its voice must be heard."

on yourself, but your conscience will demand to be heard and the only way to deal with a troubled conscience is to answer its accusations.

The first step is to try and discern between true and false guilt:

> False guilt comes when you take responsibility for something God did not call you to do or for something that was not under your control.

> True guilt comes when you shirk responsibility for something that God has called you to do or when you do what He has commanded you not to do.

The answer to false guilt is truth, and the answer to true guilt is grace. Our Lord Jesus Christ is "full of grace and truth" (John 1:14), and this means that in Him we have all we need for dealing with guilt, whether it be false or true.

> *"The answer to false guilt is truth, and the answer to true guilt is grace."*

It isn't always easy, however, to tell the difference between true and false guilt, and here's what often happens: Grieving people feel a weight of guilt. It runs deep and it is not easy for them to express. When they speak about it, they are told that they are suffering from false guilt, that it wasn't their fault, and that it is time to put this behind them and move on. This had been Leslie's experience, and the response she received had done nothing to lift the burden she carried.

After our group discussion about guilt, I offered to meet with Leslie and to help her bring the burden of guilt she was bearing before the Lord. When we met, we looked at the book of Hebrews and saw that Christ died not only so that Leslie's sins could be forgiven but also that her conscience could be cleansed.

Hebrews tells us that the blood of Christ will "purify our conscience" (Hebrews 9:14). In the light of this, God invites us to "draw near with a true heart in full assurance of faith, with our hearts sprinkled clean from an evil conscience" (10:22).

"Let's put the discussion of whether your guilt is true or false aside," I said. "What you are experiencing is real. Your conscience is burdened because you believe there is something you could or should have done 18 years ago. Now, if this was true guilt, what would you do with it?" I asked.

Leslie's answer was clear: "I would confess it to God and place it under the cleansing power of the blood of Christ."

"Well, let's do that now," I said.

Leslie took a few minutes to write down what she wanted to confess and then, for the first time, poured out to the Lord the regrets that had haunted her for years and placed them under the blood of Christ.

Some months later, Leslie spoke of what the Lord had done for her. "I came to see that whether my guilt was true or false, I needed to confess what was on my conscience and to believe that if the blood of Christ is good enough for God, it should be good enough for me. I prayed for forgiveness and laid my guilt at the cross of Christ. My conscience has been cleansed and I feel like a huge burden has been lifted from my soul."

If your conscience is burdened, I encourage you to follow Leslie's example. Write out what weighs on your conscience and bring it to God. Tell the Lord what you should have done and did not do. Tell Him what you did that you now deeply regret. Lay your "what ifs" and your "if onlys" before the Lord. Then put what you confess under the blood of Christ for the cleansing of your conscience, and ask Him to give you His peace.

"The Son of God suffered and died, not only so that your sins may be forgiven but also that your conscience may be cleansed."

You can do this on your own, or you could do this, as Leslie did, with the help of a pastor or a trusted friend. However you do it, bring your sense of guilt before the Lord. The Son of God suffered and died, not only so that your sins may be forgiven but also that your conscience may be cleansed. So don't live with a burden of guilt. Confession is a marvelous gift when you know that forgiveness, cleansing, and peace lie on the other side.

QUESTIONS FOR REFLECTION
AND DISCUSSION

1. What did you identify with in Ken and Leslie's story?

2. As you think about your loss, what would be your "what ifs" and your "if onlys?"

3. Place each of your "what ifs" and "if onlys" into the categories of true guilt, false guilt, or not sure.

4. What does it mean to you to know that God has made provision not only for the forgiveness of your sins but also for the cleansing of your conscience?

5. Sometimes confessing your guilt to the Lord does not bring about a clear conscience. Is there someone you could talk to who could encourage you in the gospel?

GRIEVANCE

GRIEVANCE

Stace and Kathy's Story

Stace and Kathy were celebrating his birthday when she told him the good news that she was pregnant. Tears of joy welled up in Stace's eyes. The joy of expecting a second child and the prospect of a brother or sister for their daughter, Emma, made their hearts overflow.

But when Kathy went for a routine checkup a few weeks later, something unusual showed up in one of the tests, indicating that the baby might have a heart condition or Down syndrome or Trisomy 18.

Neither Stace nor Kathy had ever heard of Trisomy 18, but when they came home from the appointment they began their research. "I just remember reading one sentence that said, 'Severe mental retardation, birth defects, and early death,'" Kathy said. "Those are the words that stayed with me."

Trisomy 18 was only one of three possibilities, and Stace and Kathy had been told that the chance of their baby suffering from one of these conditions was only 10%–20%.

Two weeks later, Stace and Kathy met with a specialist. "It was a bad appointment," Kathy said. "He was just there to convince us to abort." Stace and Kathy had a list of questions for the doctor, but could not get him to engage with any of them. "It would be a crime to bring this baby into the world," the doctor said.

Stace and Kathy had no interest in aborting their baby. They moved to another hospital, and from the first phone call to schedule an appointment, their experience was completely different. "We met with a genetic counselor the very first day, and they wanted us to know that they would support us regardless of what we decided to do," Stace said.

In the course of this visit, Stace and Kathy discovered that they were expecting a boy, a baby brother for their daughter, Emma.

Things were looking up. A diagnosis had not yet been made, and of the three possibilities they had been given, Stace and Kathy were hoping their baby might be suffering a hole in the heart which could easily be remedied. "A hole in the heart is not uncommon and it's not life-threatening," Kathy said. "Maybe surgery within a year! They fix it and our son lives a full life."

But when Stace and Kathy next visited the hospital, they were confronted with a harsher reality. A cardiologist spent about two-and-a-half hours studying their baby's heart which, at 20 weeks, was about the size of a dime. What he saw ruled out Down syndrome, so it was either a heart condition or Trisomy 18.

To add to Stace and Kathy's concern, an ultrasound had shown that their baby had a clubfoot, cysts in the brain, a small stomach, and a strawberry-shaped head, all consistent with Trisomy 18. "We were trying to stay hopeful and positive," Stace said. "But I started questioning what to pray for. We were both convinced that God can heal. God could cause it not to be Trisomy 18, but it seemed like the answer we were getting was 'no.'"

> *"We were trying to stay hopeful and positive, but I started questioning what to pray for."*

"For ten weeks we were praying like crazy," Kathy said, "then at our 30-week-appointment they saw clenched fists, yet another sign of Trisomy 18. And that's when we said, 'this is leading toward the worst scenario we could ever have imagined.'"

Questions flooded into Kathy's mind: *How long will my baby survive? How will this affect Emma? And if I'm going to be a grieving mother for the rest of my life, how will I be able to be the mom I want to be for her?*

"There was so much uncertainty," Stace said. "In most cases a baby with Trisomy 18 lives for a few minutes, hours, or days. Rarely does a baby with this condition live longer."

"We knew that stillbirth was a possibility," Kathy added. "We were just praying that he would make his due date, that he would be able to survive birth, that we would have time with him, and that Emma would bond with her brother."

These hopes and prayers were answered. Nathanael David was born on January 13, 2014, weighing in at 4 pounds and 9 ounces. He was given oxygen immediately after his birth, and to Stace and Kathy's joy, he soon began breathing on his own.

"One of our concerns was that we didn't know if his esophagus was connected to his stomach," Kathy said. "But after five hours, I really wanted to feed my baby, so they put a feeding tube in his nose and he did well for the first night. But by the following morning, it was difficult for Nathanael to breathe, so from that point onward, he was on oxygen. Otherwise he was doing really well, and after two days, we were able to take Nathanael home."

"The days that followed were intense in every way," Kathy said. "It was physically exhausting, trying to make the most of the time without knowing how much time we had."

Stace and Kathy established a routine in which one of them was with Nathanael around the clock. Twice in the first week they had a scare as Nathanael started gasping for air, and his color changed. "We thought he was going, but I flipped him over and he started breathing fine," Kathy said.

Stace and Kathy enjoyed 27 precious days with their son, and during that time, Emma bonded with her brother. Then, God called Nathanael home. Recalling Nathanael's last day, Kathy said, "We knew that the end was soon, so we called my family over. That night, after everyone left, we both stayed up with Nathanael, but when neither of us could keep our eyes open, I took Nathanael with me into bed and slept with him. Stace slept in 15-minute intervals so that he could check on us. At one point, he woke me and said, 'Kathy, I think he's gone.' He looked like he was sleeping peacefully, but he was cold to the touch. Nathanael died in my arms. He just slipped away."

GRIEVANCE TOWARD GOD

"It's hard to believe that God loves you when He takes away someone you love," Kathy said as she shared her story with our group. Everyone agreed, and that got us talking about grievance toward God.

> "It's hard to believe that God loves you when He takes away someone you love."

The words *grief* and *grievance* are obviously related. When you walk through grief, don't be surprised if you meet with grievance.

Grievance is the other side of guilt that we considered in the last chapter. Guilt relates to what you did or failed to do. Grievance relates to what other people did or failed to do and sometimes to what God did or failed to do.

If you have felt grievance toward God over the loss of someone you love, you are not alone. When Jesus arrived in Bethany after the death of Lazarus, the first words Martha spoke were, "Lord, if you had been here, my brother would not have died" (John 11:21). There's grievance there!

When her sister Mary finally came out to meet Jesus, she repeated the same complaint, "Lord, if you had been here, my brother would not have died," (John 11:32, see also 11:37). My guess is that what they said to Jesus was what they had been saying to each other. "Where was Jesus when our brother died? Why would He let this happen to Lazarus and to us?"

Grief invariably brings out grievance, and the second chapter of Lamentations is a sustained outpouring of complaint against God.[6] Read the verses that follow with an emphasis on the word *He* and you will catch the grievance that they felt towards the Lord:

> How *the Lord* in his anger
>> has set the daughter of Zion under a cloud!
> *He* has cast down from heaven to earth
>> the splendor of Israel;
> *he* has not remembered his footstool
>> in the day of his anger.
> *The Lord* has swallowed up without mercy
>> all the habitations of Jacob;
> in his wrath *he* has broken down
>> the strongholds of the daughter of Judah;
> *he* has brought down to the ground in dishonor
>> the kingdom and its rulers.
> *He* has cut down in fierce anger
>> all the might of Israel;
> *he* has withdrawn from them his right hand
>> in the face of the enemy;
> *he* has burned like a flaming fire in Jacob,
>> consuming all around.
> *He* has bent his bow like an enemy,
>> with his right hand set like a foe;
> *and he* has killed all who were delightful in our eyes
>> in the tent of the daughter of Zion;
> *he* has poured out his fury like fire.

The Lord has become like an enemy;
    he has swallowed up Israel;
he has swallowed up all its palaces;
    he has laid in ruins its strongholds,
and he has multiplied in the daughter of Judah
    mourning and lamentation. (Lamentations 2:1–5)

There is no attempt here to minimize God's involvement or to shield Him from blame. When God's people looked at their suffering, these people did not say, "God allowed it." They said, "God did it! God brought it about!"

Grievance toward God is not an expression of unbelief. In a profound way, it can be an expression of faith. The people who raised so many complaints against God in Lamentations were not secularists who believed

> *"Grievance toward God is not an expression of unbelief. In a profound way, it can be an expression of faith."*

that what they suffered happened by random chance. They were God's people! They knew that God is sovereign in all things, including the disaster that had befallen them. It was precisely because they believed this that they struggled with grievance toward God.

Grieving Christians face a unique problem when we suffer. When an atheist loses a loved one, he or she can say, "It's a cruel world." But Christians believe that God is sovereign, and we cannot avoid asking "Why?" If God is in control, why did He take my loved one away?

DID GOD CAUSE THIS OR DID
HE JUST LET IT HAPPEN?

We spoke at length in our group about how to handle a sense of grievance toward God. Joyce, whose story is told in chapter 2, told us that she had not felt anger toward God at the beginning, but that some months later she did.

When I asked Joyce what helped her, she said, "I stopped asking *why*. I said to myself, *I'm never going to know why this happened*, and when I accepted that, I had some peace."

But there was one question that Joyce could not shake off: "Did God cause this, or did He let it happen? I could never get anyone to give me a straight answer to that," she said.

Lamentations was open in front of us as we spoke, and Joyce had noticed that it offers a strikingly direct answer to her question. "Though he *cause* grief, he will have compassion" (Lamentations 3:32, emphasis added).

Later that evening, Joyce told me that she found this clarity helpful. "If God wanted this to happen, maybe I could accept it better, because I could say it was God's will. But if it was just a random accident, that would be even harder to bear."

"I think your instinct is exactly right," I said. "Whatever you believe about whether God caused an event or just let it happen, there are hard questions to answer. But I would rather live with questions about a God who was in control than contemplate the alternative, which is that God was passive, or that He let things slip through His fingers."

Joyce agreed. "To be passive would be the greatest cruelty and that can't be God," she said. "It's better to say, 'I don't know why, but God took her home.'"

Believing that God controls all things raises hard questions that we cannot answer. When our Lord Jesus suffered on the cross, He cried out, "Why?" (Matthew 27:46). And even to Him, heaven was silent. So when the agonized *Why?* rises from your soul, remember that Jesus has been there, and that He too had to trust the Father without being given an answer. No answer was given to the Son of God in His suffering, and we should not expect that an explanation will be given to us.

Yet there is a deep comfort that comes from knowing God controls all things. Job experienced this even in his greatest loss. He said, "The LORD gave, and the LORD has taken away" (Job 1:21).

Job's wife agreed, but the same truth that brought comfort to Job built resentment in her: "Curse God and die," she said (Job 2:9). She was saying, "I am done with this God who has brought suffering into my life, and if He exists, I would rather hate Him than trust Him."

But Job knew that to resent God would be to abandon hope: "I know that my Redeemer lives, and at the last he will stand upon the earth" (Job 19:25). He was saying, "My hope is in God, and if I were to lose faith in Him, I would lose the only hope that I have. So whatever I suffer, I will trust in Him."

When you grieve the loss of a person you love, one of these two responses will prevail in your heart. Either you will love God more or you will trust God less. Walking through the valley of sorrow will bring you closer to the Lord, or it will lock you into an ongoing battle against Him.

So how can you move beyond the grievance you may feel toward God when He takes away someone you love?

POUR OUT YOUR GRIEVANCE TO GOD

First, you need to tell God your grievance. Telling a pastor or a Christian friend that you have a grievance against God may be a good place to begin. But at some point you need to speak about this with God.

> "Lamentations models what it looks like to put your grievance into words and to pour it out in the presence of God."

Why did God breathe out a book filled with complaints and grievances against Himself? Surely it is because He wants us to bring our grievance to Him. Like many of the Psalms, Lamentations models what it looks like to put your grievance into words and to pour it out in the presence of God.

Again, a friend or pastor may be able to help you with this, but what matters most is that you tell God the truth about what you are feeling. Don't complain about God behind His back! Tell Him your grievance face-to-face. There is no better place to pour out your complaint than in the presence of God.

Eugene Peterson writes about a friend who, overwhelmed by personal, marital, and vocational troubles, began going to New York City for "scream weekends," in which sufferers are encouraged to vent accumulated anger, resentment, and pain by screaming.

The friend described his experience with enthusiasm. It was like thunder and lightning in a summer storm. He experienced a great cataclysm and then the clouds broke, giving him a wonderful feeling of peace and well-being. But while there was catharsis, there was no healing. After a few days the feeling of well-being wore off, leaving the man in need of another "scream weekend."

At one point, Peterson told his friend that it would be far healthier for him to spend a weekend shut up in a room with the book of Lamentations.[7] The friend found this incomprehensible, but Peterson was right.

Why would a weekend with Lamentations be healthier than a weekend of screaming in New York? First, because Lamentations is not a scream in the air but a cry to God, and that means that the cry is *heard*! Second, because Lamentations is better than a scream. It puts grievance into words, and pours it out, line-by-line and verse-by-verse.

There may be times in your journey through loss when there is a great deal of screaming in your soul. If that is where you are, I encourage you to do what the writer of Lamentations did: Bring your grievance to God. Tell Him what hurts you. Get it out. If you could express your grievance and bring it to God, as the sufferers in Lamentations did, it would be the beginning of your healing.

Jessica Shaver wrote a helpful poem called, "I Told God I Was Angry:"

> I told God I was angry.
> I thought He'd be surprised.
> I thought I'd kept hostility
> quite cleverly disguised.
>
> I told the Lord I hate Him.
> I told Him that I hurt.
> I told Him that He isn't fair,
> He's treated me like dirt.
>
> I told God I was angry
> But I'm the one surprised
> "What I've known all along," He said,
> "you've finally realized."
>
> "At last you have admitted
> What's really in your heart.
> Dishonesty, not anger
> was keeping us apart."
>
> "Even when you hate Me
> I don't stop loving you.
> Before you can receive that love
> you must confess what's true."
>
> "In telling Me the anger
> you genuinely feel,
> it loses power over you
> permitting you to heal."

I told God I was sorry
And He's forgiven me.
The truth that I was angry
has finally set me free.[8]

How can you move beyond the grievance you may feel toward God when He takes away someone you love? First, tell God your grievance. And second, when you bring your complaint, remember the cross.

REMEMBER "THE MAN"

One of the most striking things about Lamentations is that the grieving person who says, "He has filled me with bitterness" (Lamentations 3:15) also says, "The steadfast love of the LORD never ceases" (3:22). The same person who says, "He has made my teeth grind on gravel," (3:16), also says, "His mercies... are new every morning" (3:22–23).

How can you, in the same breath, say, "Though he cause grief, he will have compassion according to the abundance of his steadfast love" (3:32)?

The answer to that question lies in "the man:" "I am the man who has seen affliction under the rod of his [God's] wrath" (3:1).

Who is this man?

The first answer is that Jeremiah, who wrote this book, is "the man." Jeremiah suffered greatly in his life and is often referred to as the weeping prophet because of all that he endured. But there's more here than the suffering of Jeremiah and the pain of God's people in the fall of Jerusalem.

> *"There are whispers of Jesus all over Lamentations."*

There are whispers of Jesus all over Lamentations, but never more so than in these verses that clearly anticipate His suffering.

"The man" says, "My soul is bereft of peace" (3:17). And in the garden of Gethsemane, Jesus said that His soul was overwhelmed with sorrow (Mark 14:34).

"The man" says, "I have become the laughingstock of all peoples, the object of their taunts all day long" (Lamentations 3:14). And in the story of Jesus we read, "kneeling before him, they mocked him, saying, 'Hail, King of the Jews'" (Matthew 27:29).

"The man" says, "He has driven and brought me into darkness without any light" (Lamentation 3:2). And when Jesus hung on the cross, darkness covered the whole land (Matthew 27:45).

"The man" says, "Though I call and cry for help, he shuts out my prayer" (Lamentations 3:8). And this was the experience of Jesus when He cried out, "My God, my God, why have you forsaken me" (Matthew 27:46).

How extraordinary that when Jesus was put on display before the crowd, with the crown of thorns on His head, Pontius Pilate said, "Behold the man!" (John 19:5). I don't suppose he had any idea that in saying this he was pointing to how Jesus fulfilled the prophecy of Lamentations 3:1.

The good news is that God became "the man" in Jesus. God became the Man of Sorrows who is acquainted with grief. Jesus is the one who uniquely can say, "I am the man who has seen affliction under the rod of his [God's] wrath" (Lamentations 3:1).

IS GOD PUNISHING ME?

When you suffer, you may find yourself asking, "Is God punishing me?" And when you read the book of Lamentations, you might be tempted to conclude that He is.

The grieving people in Lamentations suffered because of persistent and grievous sin over many generations. For years the prophets had called the people to repent and warned of coming judgment, but their words were ignored.

Without question, the destruction of Jerusalem came about because of the judgment of God. So if their suffering was a punishment for their sins, could it be that what we suffer is punishment for our sins?

This question might sound stark, but it needs to be addressed because it often gnaws at the back of a grieving person's mind. Sometimes it comes out, usually with great hesitation: "Pastor, do you think that God might be... punishing me?" The many times I have heard that question suggest to me that this is an unspoken anxiety in the minds of many.

Let me be absolutely clear: If you are in Christ, God is not punishing you. And here's how you can be sure: God poured out His wrath at the cross. It was spent and exhausted on Jesus. There is no punishment left for you (Romans 8:1).

Jesus bore the wrath that was due to us. The punishment that brought us peace was on Him (Isaiah 53:5). He became the propitiation for our sins (Romans 3:25). "Since, therefore, we have now been justified by his blood, much more shall we be saved by him from the wrath of God" (5:9).

If you are in Christ, you may find yourself in great darkness, but you will never be under the rod of God's wrath. Jesus endured the wrath so that you would never know what that is like. He is "the man" who was afflicted by the rod of God's wrath, and He endured this for you.

Knowing this matters, because if you think that God is punishing you, resentment toward God will grow in your heart. But if you truly believe that God loves you, you won't remain angry with Him for long.

So when you feel grievance toward God, try to let these truths settle in your mind: God is for you. God is with you. His grace is sufficient. His mercies are new every morning. God is not punishing you. His heart is tender towards you. Jesus laid down His life so that God's mercy should reach you and God's love should hold you, even in your greatest loss. "There is therefore now no condemnation for those who are in Christ Jesus" (Romans 8:1).

DOES GOD REALLY LOVE ME?

These truths were life-giving for Stace and for Kathy as they fought their way through the grievance they felt over the death of their son Nathanael.

> *"If you believe that God is angry with you, it won't be long before you are angry with Him."*

"If you believe that God is angry with you, it won't be long before you are angry with Him," Kathy said. "This was one of my biggest struggles through the whole grief journey. Does God really love me?"

I reminded Kathy of what she had said in our group: "It is hard to believe that God loves you when He takes away someone you love." What had helped her in this struggle? I wanted to know.

"There are times in the Christian life when we know the love of God by faith and by feeling, but there are times when we will hang onto the love of God by faith only," she said.

"At times it was a battle to believe that God loved me. You know it from what you read in Scripture; you know it from the songs you sing; but, you don't *feel* it when you are grieving so deeply."

"So what did you do?" I asked.

"I had to keep coming back to the gospel," she answered. "I would ask myself, how can I doubt God's love for me when He gave up His Son to save me? I'm grieving the loss of my son and God gave up *His* Son for me! How can I not believe that God loves me when the thing I am grieving is what God chose to do to save me!"

I was struck by the way Kathy said, she had to "keep coming back" to the gospel. "It's a constant battle," she explained, "because you don't feel it, but when you're drowning in sorrow, you just have to find your way to that truth."

"What brought joy back into my life was reminding myself of who I am in Christ and learning to seek what He has called me to do, knowing that what He has for me each day is sovereignly and lovingly ordained for me."

"It took me two years before I could go through Nathanael's room and sort out his things, and there was a long stretch of time where I struggled every morning to start my day. When I asked, *What do I have to do today?* The answer that came to mind was not what I wanted. I longed to care for two children, not one.

"When I let my day be defined by my role as a mother, I struggled to start my day. I should have been caring for Nathanael, but I couldn't because he wasn't with me. So I felt as if I had failed before I even started. But when I began to let my day be defined by who I am in Christ, my question changed from, *What do I have to do today?* to, *Lord, what do You have in store for me today? Give me the strength to be faithful to You today.*"

In the months that followed the death of Nathanael, Stace and Kathy ploughed through the struggle she expressed so clearly to our group: "It is hard to believe that God loves you when He takes away someone you love." But looking through their grief to the Son of God who gave Himself for them, Stace and Kathy came to this conclusion: It's hard *not* to believe that God loves you when you are looking at the cross.

QUESTIONS FOR REFLECTION AND DISCUSSION

1. At what points did you relate to Stace and Kathy's experience of grief?

2. Do you feel that grievance toward God is an expression of unbelief or faith? Why?

3. Have you ever tried to articulate (write or pray) your grievance with God? What happened?

4. What is your reaction to "the man who has seen affliction under the rod of his [God's] wrath" (Lamentations 3:1)?

5. Which question has been more difficult for you in your grief: Is God punishing me? Does God really love me? Why?

HOPE

HOPE

Betty and Kristen's Story

Kristen was driving on Interstate 290 as she made her way to Rush University Medical Center where she worked as a staff nurse in the cardiac intensive care unit. It was 6:30 in the morning—just another day.

As she reached the ramp to leave the interstate, she noticed a call on her cell phone from Canada where her sister Beth was living with her husband.

Without Bluetooth in the car, Kristen kept her hands on the wheel and ignored the call. But Beth kept calling and texting. "Call me ASAP!"

"It made no sense to me," Kristen said. "Why was she calling me at this time in the morning?"

When her car was safely parked, Kristen called her sister. "What's up?" she asked curiously.

"You don't know?" Beth replied.

"Know what?"

"Kristen, Dad and John have both been killed."

Two weeks earlier, Kristen's mom and dad, Betty and Gary, had left on a trip to visit with their son John, his wife, and one-year-old daughter. The family met up at a resort in the Middle East, and then went on to Central Asia where John taught computer science at a university.

The trip had gone well, and just two days remained before Gary and Betty were due to return to Chicago. The plan for that day was to visit a local hospital where a family friend was volunteering and then to go sightseeing and shopping.

Security was tight, so when the family arrived they had to go through a checkpoint that consisted of two small huts, one for men and the other for women.

"I call them frisking huts," Betty said. "They were only a few feet square, just enough space for a couple of people at a time."

Gary and John had already gone through, as had John's wife, and Betty was in the process of being searched when she heard the sound of a gun firing over and over again.

With the door closed, Betty was unable to see what was going on, but in her heart she knew what had happened. "While the gun was still firing, the Lord said to me, 'Betty, you are a widow now,' and I said, 'Yes, Lord.'"

A few minutes later Betty heard the voice of her daughter-in-law, who had been seriously wounded in the shooting but had managed to crawl back into the men's frisking hut next door.

"Mom, Dad and John are gone," she said.

Three years after her traumatic double bereavement, I asked Betty to describe her journey through grief.

"I think I was in shock for about three months," Betty said. "There wasn't a lot of emotion. You are just numb. You move through your day like a robot. You do what you have to do, and then you do the next thing."

"For the first year, I felt overwhelmed with everything I had to do. A friend would stop over to help me with my finances. But before we were done, I would have to take a break and I would just sit and cry."

Betty's grief came in waves. "It comes unexpectedly," she said. "I was at a bridal shower, and while the bride was opening her gifts, the eldest son of the groom's family walked in. He was tall and bearded, just like John, and he was carrying a baby, about six months old. I just started to sob."

"You never know how many jobs require two people until you are alone," she continued. "Last week I was stripping the bed and decided to flip the mattress. I couldn't do it. When you are married your teammate is there, and you work together. But now I am responsible for everything. I get to make all the decisions, but that's not what I want!"

> *"You never know how many jobs require two people until you are alone."*

When I asked Betty about the role of friends in her life, she offered this helpful insight: "After my tragedy, a lot of people wanted to minister to me, and in some cases they were people I didn't know well. But this just isn't a time to be making new friends. It's a time you want to be surrounded by the people you are already close with."

Over these years, Betty has learned that she does not need to share her sorrow with everyone who asks. "People will often ask how I am doing, but it's not always the right time or place to get into that conversation. I am learning to redirect the topic of conversation at those times."

"You need to allow some people into your sorrow, but it needs to be the right people and it needs to be the right time. That's one reason why our grief group was so helpful. Being with people I knew who had also experienced great loss gave me a safe place to process my sorrows. I can't say enough about how helpful that was."

"Now I have to find a new life," Betty said. "That's my challenge, and it isn't easy." Her voice broke as she continued, "I grieve with hope every day."

What does it mean to grieve with hope? And how is it possible?

GRIEVING WITH HOPE

In 1 Thessalonians, the Apostle Paul says:

> We do not want you to be uninformed, brothers, about those who are asleep, that you may not grieve as others do who have no hope. (4:13)

These words have sometimes been misunderstood by Christians who take them to mean that believers should not grieve because we have hope. But the contrast Paul is making is not between grief and hope, as if these were alternatives. It is between believers, who have hope when we grieve, and unbelievers, who do not.

Paul is not saying that if you have hope you will not grieve. He is saying that when you grieve, you have hope because you will be reunited with believing loved ones when Christ comes again.

Grief without hope is the experience of those who do not believe that Jesus rose from the dead. For them, death brings a final separation from their loved ones. They may look back on fond memories, but cannot look forward to the joy of seeing their loved ones again.

But our grief is not like that. We grieve, but not like those who have no hope. Our grief is different: "We believe that Jesus died and rose again" and so we believe that "God will bring with him those who have fallen asleep" (1 Thessalonians 4:14).

> *"We grieve, but not like those who have no hope."*

Death was not the end for Jesus, and it will not be the end for those who have died in Him. Your believing loved one is with Christ, and when Jesus comes again they will be with Him.

When you are grieving the loss of a believing loved one, you can find hope, comfort, strength, and encouragement in these five wonderful truths:

1. The soul of your believing loved one is at home with the Lord (2 Corinthians 5:8).

2. When our Lord returns, He will bring your believing loved one with Him (1 Thessalonians 4:14).

3. At that time, your loved one will receive the gift of a new body like the risen body of Jesus (1 Corinthians 15:51–52).

4. If you are still living when that day comes, your body will be instantaneously changed and adapted for the new and everlasting life that lies ahead of you (1 Corinthians 15:51–52).

5. In that resurrection body, you will see Jesus Christ face to face, and in His presence you will be reunited with your believing loved one forever (1 Thessalonians 4:17–18).

Think about what this will mean for Gary and John. When they were murdered, their souls were brought into the immediate, conscious enjoyment of the presence of the Lord. But Gary and John's bodies are not with the Lord. Their bodies were taken from the hospital grounds, flown back to the United States, and laid to rest.

When the Lord returns, He will bring the souls of Gary and John with Him, and then they will receive the gift of the resurrection body. Viewed from heaven, their souls will come down with Jesus. Viewed from the earth, their bodies will be raised to life with Jesus.

Gary and John will then have the joy of being reunited with their believing loved ones in a new and everlasting chapter of the life they already enjoy with the Lord.

If Betty and Kristen are alive when Christ returns, they will have the joy of being reunited with Gary and John on that day. This is what Paul means when he says:

We who are alive [that is, people who are still living when the Lord returns]... will be caught up together with them [that is, caught up with our believing loved ones who have died and are already with Jesus]. (1 Thessalonians 4:17)

The great future hope for all Christians in sorrow and loss is that when we see Christ, we will see our believing loved ones again.

FOR PARENTS WHO LOST CHILDREN EARLY

What will this mean for parents whose children died in infancy?

All of God's children will be made perfect in the presence of Jesus. We will all reach the full measure of our redeemed power and potential. Each of us will be all that God created and redeemed us to be.

Children who die in infancy will not be eternal infants, and those who die after an extended life, in which their later years may have been marked by frailty and dementia, will not be eternally frail or forgetful.

This is a very wonderful truth for parents who have lost a child and often wonder what he or she would have become if they had grown into the full maturity of adult life. Well, one day you will find out.

How great will be Joyce and Wayne's joy when they see all that Jill, who they lost at the age of two, has become in the full beauty of her redeemed womanhood! How great will Stace and Kathy's joy be when they see all that Nathanael, who they held for just 27 days, has become in the full strength of his redeemed manhood!

If you grieve over a miscarriage, or if you have endured the unspeakable sorrow of losing a child, you will see your son or daughter again. And when you see what he or she has become, you will be overwhelmed with joy. Until then, we grieve. But we grieve with hope.

HOPE FOR TODAY

Having walked through the conversations about tears, talk, guilt, and grievance, I had looked forward to our group talking about heaven. We had a good conversation, but compared with our other discussions, I felt that this one didn't really take off.

Looking back I can see why. The fulfillment of God's ultimate purpose is very wonderful, and every Christian needs to know it. But heaven may seem a long way from the painful realities that a grieving person faces every day. The immediate question, especially in the early stages of a journey through grief is often, "How am I going to get through today?" And heaven is not the answer to that question.

> *"Heaven may seem a long way from the painful realities that a grieving person faces every day."*

Charles Spurgeon often endured extended bouts of depression. He knew from his own experience that heaven can seem remote to a person in great darkness. And he found that afflicted people often derive more comfort from Christ's first coming than they do from the hope of our Lord's return.

Zack Eswine explains why: In His first coming, Christ came as a weary man and full of woes, and "we ourselves are weary and full of woe, with no finishing line in sight."[9]

The marathon runner needs more than the anticipation of joy at the end of the journey. He or she needs strength to keep pressing forward through the grueling miles that still lie ahead. Family and friends may cheer and shout "we'll see you at the finish," but for the runner, the real question is "how do I get through the next mile?"

Perhaps that is why the focus in Lamentations is not on our hope for tomorrow, but on the hope and help that God gives to grieving people today.

A PORTRAIT OF GRIEF

In the central and best known chapter of Lamentations, Jeremiah paints a portrait of grief that all who have walked the valley of sorrow and loss will recognize:

1. You find yourself in darkness.

He has driven and brought me into darkness without any light. (Lamentations 3:2)

When you are in darkness, you can't see what is ahead of you, you don't know what is around you, and you lose sight of what is behind you. Darkness is disorienting. Without fixed points of reference, you don't know where you are.

2. You feel trapped.

He has walled me about so that I cannot escape. (3:7)

Bereavement feels like being in prison. You know that there is a world of freedom and light that others are enjoying, but you can't get there. You feel trapped by the loss you have suffered.

3. You feel weighed down.

He has made my chains heavy. (3:7)

Friends try to interest you in getting out and doing things, but nothing appeals to you. You don't have the energy, and you don't see the point. Everything seems like an overwhelming effort. You don't want to get up, don't want to eat, and don't want to talk. And when you drag yourself into activity, you wonder if it is worth it.

4. You feel afraid.

He is a bear lying in wait for me, a lion in hiding. (3:10)

If your loss has taken you by surprise, you may find yourself wondering what other disasters lie ahead. Jeremiah uses the image of a waiting bear and a hidden lion to express this fear. What will happen next?

5. You feel foolish.

I have become the laughingstock of all peoples. (3:14)

Your loss has made you the focus of attention. The eyes of other people are on you, and you often wonder what they think. Do they think you should be doing better? Making more progress? Showing more faith? Suddenly you find that you have to do things you did not do before.

Other people know how to do them, but to you, they are unfamiliar. So you feel foolish, and you fear that others may think you're foolish too.

6. You feel miserable.

> My soul is bereft of peace; I have forgotten what happiness is. (3:17)

Bereft of peace means you are always on edge, you are never comfortable, and you never really rest. You try to draw comfort from the memories of happy times, but remembering only reinforces your loss. Happiness is far from where you are now, and you can't imagine it ever returning.

7. You feel exhausted.

> "My endurance has perished; so has my hope from the LORD." (3:18)

Grief is exhausting. It drains the life out of you leaving you constantly tired and lacking motivation. Worst of all, you feel that you have lost hope. God seems far from you, and you fear He may have forgotten you.

I'm in darkness. I'm trapped. I'm weighed down. I'm afraid. I feel foolish. I feel miserable. I'm exhausted. That's a portrait of grief that all who walk the valley of sorrow and loss will recognize.

If you endure times when you cannot remember what it was like to be happy, remember that other grieving Christians have been there, and that they did not remain there. If you have days when you lose hope, it will help you to know that when other believers said "my hope has perished," it was not their final word.

Knowing that a Christian's experience of grief can sometimes bring great darkness, and that a believer may even lose sight of hope for a time, will help you not to be taken by surprise if this should happen to you. Other believers have been there and God has brought them through.

What is truly remarkable is that the same person who said, "My hope has perished" (3:18) also says, "I have hope" (3:21) and "I will hope" (3:24). How is that possible?

THE JOURNEY TO HOPE

Jeremiah says, "But this I call to mind and therefore I have hope" (Lamentations 3:21). What in the world could a person who has endured unspeakable sorrow call to mind that would bring them hope when they have forgotten what happiness is?

If you asked me to guess what comes next, I would expect the promise of a better future. After all, that's what happened. Seventy years after Jerusalem was destroyed, the city was rebuilt in the time of Ezra and Nehemiah. And God had already revealed that one day there will be a new Jerusalem, a city made perfect where there will be no more sorrow, crying, or pain (Isaiah 65:17–21; Revelation 21:1–4). So Jeremiah could easily have written, "But this I call to mind and therefore I have hope: There will be a New Jerusalem, and God will wipe all tears from our eyes."

> *"Heaven is a promise for tomorrow, and what you need is strength for today."*

But that is not what God says in Lamentations.

In the depth of their sorrow, God's people were not thinking with joyful anticipation about their future hope. Heaven is a promise for tomorrow, and what you need is strength for today.

So what can you call to mind when your soul continually remembers your loss and is bowed down within you?

> But this I call to mind,
> and therefore I have hope:
> The steadfast love of the LORD never ceases;
> his mercies never come to an end;
> they are new every morning;
> great is your faithfulness.
> "The LORD is my portion," says my soul,
> "therefore I will hope in him." (Lamentations 3:21–24)

Notice the things that we must call to mind:

1. The steadfast love of the LORD never ceases.

When everything else is shifting, God's love for you remains the same. It is steadfast. The love of God for you had no beginning, and it will have no end. You are loved with an everlasting love (Jeremiah 31:3). And this love is proved beyond all doubt at the cross.

2. His mercies never come to an end; they are new every morning.

God's mercies are His kindness that will always provide what you need. God knows every tear you shed, and every fear that passes through your mind. As each new day unfolds, God will give you what you need to face it. "As your days, so shall your strength be" (Deuteronomy 33:25).

> *"Christ will give you the strength you need to match the load you carry at any given time."*

Paul said, "I can do everything through Christ, who gives me strength" (Philippians 4:13, NLT). Notice the word "gives." Christ will give you the strength you need to match the load you carry at any given time. When He doubles your load, He can also double your strength. God knows what you are facing, and He will give you an infusion of strength to match every need of every hour.

3. "The LORD is my portion," says my soul, "therefore I will hope in him."

Your "portion" is what you are given. The natural inclination of a grieving person is to focus on what you have lost. But faith focuses on what you have, and what you have in your journey through sorrow is God Himself. Your hope as a Christian believer in the pain of your sorrow and loss is that God will walk with you, His love will not fail you, and His mercies will be new every morning.

A TUG-OF-WAR

Hope lies in the faithfulness of God, but it is not easy to fix in your mind the great truth of God's steadfast love. Jeremiah models what this looks like: "But this I call to mind, and therefore I have hope" (Lamentations 3:21). This calling to mind involves a deliberate and repeated effort by a grieving person who feels weighed down, trapped, afraid, and exhausted but refuses to give in. He hauls his mind from what he has lost to what he has, knowing that his hope is in God alone.

Picture a woman in a canoe that is being carried by whitewater rapids. She has lost her paddle, and she has no means of resisting the current that is taking her toward an abyss. Then she sees a tree that has fallen over the river. Here is something to which she can hold, so she grabs the tree and clings to it, knowing that her life depends upon it.

That's what calling to mind the love and mercy of God is like. When the whitewater rapids of grief are carrying you away, the everlasting love of God is the tree of life to which you must cling. Calling God's love and mercy to mind so that you find hope in Him will not be easy when you are in the depth of sorrow. But it is possible.

Kristen knows what it is to fight this battle. "It's a tug-of-war," she said. "The grieving and the hope, it's back and forth. It can be a struggle. But when you do this successfully, you will not be consumed by negative thoughts."

I love Kristen's picture because a tug of war means you are pulling on the rope even if sometimes you are losing ground. So I asked Kristen, what helped her pull on the rope? What gives her hope?

"You have to drip-feed the truth into your brain," she said. "The promises that help me are the eternal ones. One day this suffering will be over. I will see my dad and my brother again. I also find it helpful to think about the suffering our Lord went through. It takes a lot of conscious effort to slow down and think about what the cross means," she continued, "but I find that it gives me the perspective that I need."

Betty agrees. "I had so much to do, and I couldn't have done what I did without the Lord. But the Holy Spirit was with me, and He got me through."

> *"A tug-of-war means you are pulling on the rope even if sometimes you are losing ground."*

The verses we have pondered in this chapter describe a remarkable journey. The same person who said, "I'm in darkness, I'm trapped, I'm weighed down, I'm afraid, I feel foolish, I feel miserable, and I'm exhausted," was also able to say, "The LORD is my portion, therefore I will hope in him" (3:24). The same person who said "my hope has perished" found that hope was renewed when he called to mind the love, mercy, and faithfulness of God.

On the first anniversary of the deaths of Gary and John, I had the privilege of leading a short service for a small circle of family and friends. Betty had asked for a simple service that included some readings and prayers, along with words of encouragement spoken by friends who stood with the family beside the graves of their loved ones.

After several friends had spoken, there was a pause, and I sensed that the time had come to bring the service to a close. I was in the process of thanking those who had come when Betty indicated that she would like to say a few words. No one who was present will ever forget what she said: "Over the last year, many people have asked me about the day that changed my life. The day Gary and John died has surely changed my life, but the day that changed my life forever was the day that I received Jesus Christ as my Savior and Lord."

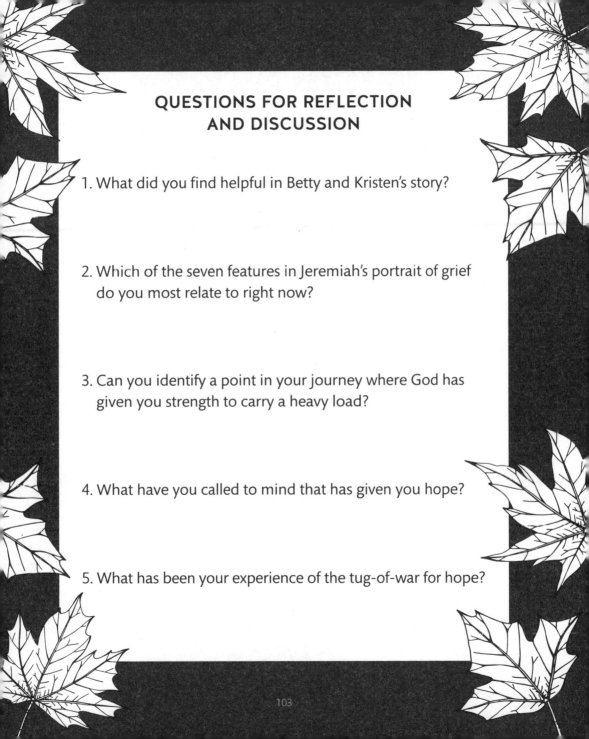

QUESTIONS FOR REFLECTION
AND DISCUSSION

1. What did you find helpful in Betty and Kristen's story?

2. Which of the seven features in Jeremiah's portrait of grief do you most relate to right now?

3. Can you identify a point in your journey where God has given you strength to carry a heavy load?

4. What have you called to mind that has given you hope?

5. What has been your experience of the tug-of-war for hope?

HEALING

HEALING

Come with me and sit with the people whose sorrow and loss gave rise to the book of Lamentations. Many of them had lost children, and on top of that they had lost their homes and their freedom.

As each new day began, they looked out over the ruins of their once great city. Jerusalem, which the prophets had praised as the joy of all the earth, had been reduced to a heap of rubble. Numbed by their suffering and lost for words, God's people sat in silence.

Only in the last chapter of the book do we hear them speak: "Remember, O LORD, what has befallen us" (Lamentations 5:1). Notice the word "us." At last these people, who have suffered devastating loss, are able to speak.

How did they get there? Through the ministry of the person who speaks in the first four chapters.

Lamentations was written under the inspiration of the Holy Spirit by the prophet Jeremiah. He ministered to grieving people in their sorrow and loss, and his ministry is a model of counseling at its best.

God gave His people a counselor who wept with them, put the pain of their loss into words, ministered to their guilt and grief, and brought hope and healing from the ashes of their loss.

What God did for His grieving people through the counseling ministry of Jeremiah anticipates what He is able to do for you through Jesus Christ in your grief and sorrow.

A COUNSELOR WHO WEEPS WITH YOU

Picture yourself sitting with a counselor who is helping you, supporting you, and guiding you through your grief and loss. He is not sitting behind a desk. He is beside you in your sorrow, and he weeps with you.

Your head is in your hands as you mourn over the smoldering ruins of your home, and the counselor says: "How lonely sits the city that was full of people!" (Lamentations 1:1). The counselor is not a detached observer. He is in the grief with you. Your city is his city, your loss is his loss, your sorrow is his sorrow.

Verse by verse and line by line, the counselor holds up the shattered pieces of your broken life and puts what you cannot express into words: "Here's what you've felt. Here's what you've lost. Here's what you've experienced."

When the counselor speaks, he expresses what you are thinking and feeling so precisely that you begin to wonder, *How does he know me so fully and completely?*

As you walk through bereavement, you may have felt that no one could ever know the extent of your grief and sorrow. But what if there is a counselor who feels all that you have felt, sees all that you have seen, and knows all that you have experienced?

You may say, "That is impossible! No one can ever know my mind, my heart, and all that has happened in my life." But Lamentations is telling us that when the people of God were at a place

> *"What if there is a counselor who feels all that you have felt, sees all that you have seen, and knows all that you have experienced?"*

so dark and so desperate that they could not speak for themselves, someone came. And he wept with them and spoke to them as one who knew their suffering from the inside.

Jesus Christ is the Counselor who comes alongside us (Isaiah 9:6), and He does this by His Holy Spirit (John 14:16). God's Spirit is with you, and He lives in you (John 14:17). So He knows all that you have ever felt and thought from the inside.

A COUNSELOR WHO SPEAKS TO YOU

Picture this counselor, who has been sitting beside you, describing all that you have thought or felt. Now, he pulls up a chair and sits down opposite you, and looking deep into your eyes, he speaks to you about himself.[10] A relationship has been established, and he wants you to know him as he already knows you.

The counselor introduces himself as "the man who has seen affliction" (Lamentations 3:1). He tells you that he has suffered under the rod of God's wrath (3:1), that he was driven into darkness without any light

(3:2), that he was mocked and taunted (3:14), that he could not find peace (3:17), that he knows what it is to cry out to God and receive no answer (3:8).

As the counselor describes his experience, you can see that he knows your suffering from the inside and, as you listen to him speak, you sense that he can do more than sympathize over your loss. This counselor is able to *help* you in your journey through sorrow and loss.

THE COUNSELOR WILL HELP YOU TO PRAY

As we saw earlier, the ministry of the counselor in Lamentations continues for four chapters. In all this time, the people do not speak a single word. The counselor speaks for them. All they are able to do is listen to his words. But in chapter 5, God's grieving people finally speak for themselves: "Remember, O LORD, what has befallen us" (Lamentations 5:1).[11]

Notice that their first words are spoken to God. At last, these people who have been drowning in grief are able to pray, and it is the ministry of the counselor that has brought them there.

As you walk through grief, you may feel that God is far from you. You may find it difficult to pray, and when you try, you may wonder if God hears you at all.

If you feel that God is beyond your reach, remember that godly people have been there before. At one point in his journey through grief, C. S. Lewis wrote: "Meanwhile where is God?... Go to Him when your need is desperate, when all other help is vain, and what do you find? A door slammed in your face, and a sound of bolting and double bolting on the inside. After that, silence."[12]

God's people in Lamentations felt like that. But God did not abandon them. He sent a counselor whose patient ministry of the Word brought God's grieving people to the place where they were able to pray.

If you read through Lamentations 5, you will see that, far from being a beautifully composed prayer, it is a visceral outpouring of a soul in deep pain. And that tells us something important: You don't need to have an ordered and peaceful mind before you can pray.

"You don't need to have an ordered and peaceful mind before you can pray."

When Hannah prayed, "she was deeply distressed… and wept bitterly" (1 Samuel 1:10). When Jesus prayed in the Garden of Gethsemane, His soul was overwhelmed with sorrow (Mark 14:34). So be encouraged by this: You don't have to be calm, confident, and clear-minded before you can draw near to God in prayer. Come to God as you are and say it like it is. The Father will hear you, and the Holy Spirit will help you, as you offer your prayer in the name of Jesus.

THE COUNSELOR WILL SUSTAIN YOUR FAITH

After all of their grief, and despite all of their unanswered questions, the faith of God's people remained. True faith is not an escape from reality.

It is the gift that equips us to face reality in a world scarred by pain, sorrow, and loss.

Lamentations plumbs the depths of grief from beginning to end. There is no evasion of the heartache, no downplaying of the pain, no trite assertions that everything will be all right. At the end of the book, God's people are still saying, "The joy of our hearts has ceased; our dancing has been turned to mourning" (Lamentations 5:15).

But the ministry of the counselor brings them to a place where they can also say:

> But you, O LORD, reign forever;
> your throne endures to all generations. (Lamentations 5:19)

After all that these people had endured, that's amazing!

God's people are looking at their city and its temple in ruins. And yet they have been brought by the counselor to a place where they know that God's rule doesn't depend on a city or on a temple. God reigns! And He advances His great purpose even in the worst of circumstances.

Reflecting on the stories that Lyle and Sue, Wayne and Joyce, Ken and Leslie, Stace and Kathy, and Betty and Kristen have shared in this book, I am overwhelmed by this single thought: Here are people who have experienced excruciating pain. Their loss remains. None of them has an answer to the question "Why?" Yet all of them love Jesus!

If their faith was simply a human decision, their pain and loss would surely have led them to renounce their faith and move in a different direction.

So why is it that people who live with unanswered questions, prolonged illness, dashed hopes and dreams still love Christ and still believe?

There can only be one explanation. Faith is a living seed and it is indestructible.

Think about the experience of a bulb planted in the ground. The gardener takes the bulb and places it in a perfectly-shaped hole that holds it like a cradle. Then the gardener pours dirt over the bulb and buries it completely! But the bulb grows where it is planted, and the dirt piled over it actually contributes to its growth.

Walking through bereavement, you may feel buried by all that had been dumped on you, and you may wonder how your faith could ever survive. But Lamentations reminds us that God sustains the faith of His people even in the worst of circumstances.

Your faith holds onto Christ, but the greater truth is that Christ holds onto you. An old hymn says it well: "When I fear my faith will fail, Christ will hold me fast." Christ died to save you, He lives to keep you, and His love will never let you go.

> *"Your faith holds onto Christ, but the greater truth is that Christ holds onto you."*

As you listen to His Word, and as He walks with you in your sorrow, Christ, the Counselor, will bring you to a place where you are able to say, "But you, O LORD, reign forever; your throne endures to all generations" (Lamentations 5:19).

THE COUNSELOR WILL RENEW YOUR HOPE

After pouring out the agony of their hearts, God's people say, "Restore us to yourself, O Lord, that we may be restored!" (Lamentations 5:21).

If they had simply said, "Restore us to yourself, O Lord," we would rightly describe that as a prayer. But there's more here: "Restore us to yourself, O Lord, *that we may be restored!*"

That's a statement of hope. These people are saying, "Lord, if you bring us back to yourself, we can face anything. Whatever happens, there is hope for us so long as we have You!" Or to put it in New Testament terms, "If God is for us, who can be against us?" (Romans 8:31). God's people are convinced that if God restores them, they will be in an entirely different position. That's hope, and the ministry of the counselor has brought them there.

When Jesus says, "I am the resurrection and the life" (John 11:25), He offers hope for the believer who has died and hope for the believer who lives. Christ is the resurrection, and that means there is a glorious future for every believer who has died. Your loved one is safe with Christ. Right now, the life they enjoy is better than anything they could ever have known here. And still to come for them is the day of resurrection when all of God's people will be given bodies adapted for eternal life in the redeemed creation that one day we will all enjoy.

But Christ also says, "I am the life," and this promise is especially for you as you grieve. Losing a loved one can drain your will to live, but when Christ says, "I am the life," He reminds you that He is your reason for living, and He will give you all that you need for the life that lies ahead of you.

The ministry of the counselor brought the grieving people in Lamentations to a place where they could pray, trust, and hope. And what the counselor did for them, Jesus is able to do for you.

QUESTIONS THAT REMAIN

God's people knew that God *could* restore Jerusalem, but they did not know if He *would*.

Faith lives with questions.

The same people who prayed, "Restore us to yourself, O LORD, that we may be restored" go on to say, "... unless you have utterly rejected us, and you remain exceedingly angry with us" (Lamentations 5:21-22). There are lingering question here: Has God rejected us? Will God remain angry with us forever?

Jesus is the answer to the questions at the end of Lamentations. God sent His Son into the world. God became "the man," and, on the cross, He suffered affliction under the rod of divine wrath in our place. God has reconciled us to Himself in Jesus Christ (2 Corinthians 5:19).

Would it have been better if Lamentations had ended on a note of triumph? "Restore us to yourself, O LORD, that we may be restored" seems like a perfect ending for the book of Lamentations. Why spoil it by adding "unless you have utterly rejected us, and you remain exceedingly angry with us?" Isn't that a letdown?

> *"People who pray, trust, and hope still have questions."*

God makes no mistakes, and Lamentations has exactly the right ending. Grief is never neat and tidy. People who pray, trust, and hope still have questions. We walk by faith, not by sight. One day, faith will be turned to sight, but that day has not yet come. Until it does, we will have questions. The last verse of Lamentations guards against premature closure.

As your journey through grief continues, people may ask you if you are "getting over it," sometimes with little understanding of the ongoing effects of grief and loss. C. S. Lewis comments:

> To say the patient is "getting over it" after an operation for appendicitis is one thing; after he's had his leg off it is quite another. After that operation either the wounded stump heals or the man dies. If it heals, the fierce continuous pain will stop. Presently he'll get back his strength and be able to stump about on his wooden leg. He has "got over it." But he will probably have recurrent pains in the stump all his life... and he will always be a one-legged man.[13]

So what does healing look like when you are enduring an irreplaceable loss? How would you know that you are making progress? Look for the fruit of the Counselor's ministry in your life. *Am I praying more? Am I trusting more? Do I see the beginnings of hope?*

Don't expect that all your questions will be answered, or that all your fears will vanish, or that all your sorrows will be gone. But you can be sure of this: Jesus Christ your Counselor, who knows your suffering from the inside, will walk with you. And, over time, He will bring you to a place where you are able to pray, and to trust, and to hope.

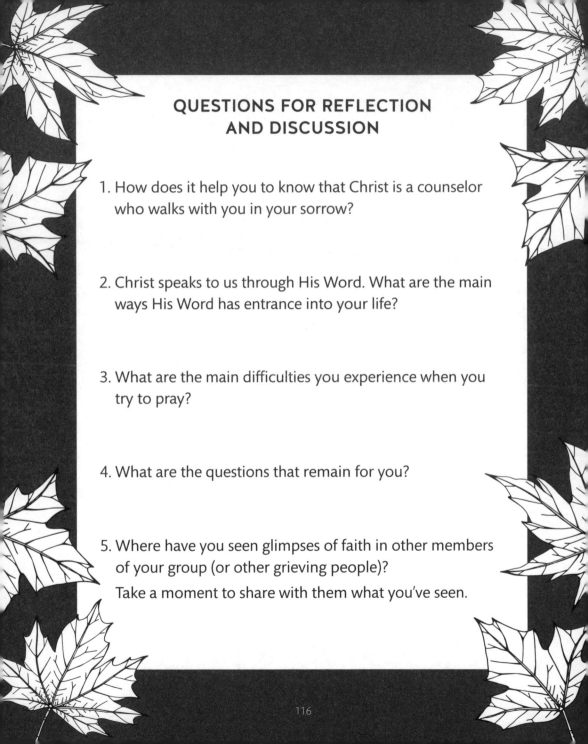

QUESTIONS FOR REFLECTION AND DISCUSSION

1. How does it help you to know that Christ is a counselor who walks with you in your sorrow?

2. Christ speaks to us through His Word. What are the main ways His Word has entrance into your life?

3. What are the main difficulties you experience when you try to pray?

4. What are the questions that remain for you?

5. Where have you seen glimpses of faith in other members of your group (or other grieving people)?
   Take a moment to share with them what you've seen.

POSTSCRIPT

Early in the twentieth century, a pastor in London by the name of J. Stuart Holden purchased two tickets for the maiden voyage of a new ship that many people were talking about at the time.

Shortly before the ship was due to sail, Holden's wife took ill, and to their great disappointment, the couple had to cancel their trip.

The name of the ship on which they had hoped to sail was the Titanic.[14]

When the ship sank, Holden and his wife saw the hand of God in the illness that mercifully had saved their lives. So Holden framed his unused tickets for the Titanic and underneath inscribed the words, "A Testimony to the Love of God."

When visitors came to his home, Holden would show them the tickets and tell the story of how, in God's kindness, his life was saved through the illness of his wife.

But on one occasion, when Holden was telling the story, his guest raised a question. Looking at the words that were written under the tickets, the guest said, "This is a very moving story, but I think you have the wrong inscription."

"How so?" Holden asked. "These tickets are a marvelous testimony to the love of God."

"Yes, but I have a friend who *did* sail on the Titanic," his guest replied. "He was an evangelist from Glasgow called Harper. He was on his way to preach the gospel in America, but he died in the water."

"Now, tell me Mr. Holden," said the guest, "when you say, 'a testimony to the love of God,' are you telling me that God loved you more than He loved Harper?"

Holden had no answer, except to ask, "What should I have written?"

"You should have written 'a testimony to the sovereignty of God.' God called Harper home, and God called you to remain here. Why it was that way round and not the other, you will never be able to explain."

Here were two wonderful servants of God, Harper and Holden. The love of God toward both was exactly the same. But in the mystery of God's sovereign will, one was called up quickly to heaven, and the other was left to serve longer on earth.

When you think about your loved one who has been called home, you may wonder: *Why was he or she called home? And why am I left here?*

Only God knows.

But here is what you must hold onto: God wants you here. He calls you to live in a way that honors Him. And with His help, you will.

APPENDIX

Children Who Die in Infancy

What happens to children who die in infancy? And what about the millions of lives that began in the womb but did not come to birth?

The place to begin is with the baby born to King David who died in infancy. David pleaded that God would spare the life of the child but when the baby died, David said, "I shall go to him, but he will not return to me" (2 Samuel 12:23). David knew that his son was safe in the presence of God and that one day they would be reunited.

Parents who grieve the loss of a child can also lean on the words of Jesus: "Let the children come to me; do not hinder them, for to such belongs the kingdom of God" (Mark 10:14). Jesus was speaking here about infants, and He says that the kingdom of God belongs to them.

On another occasion, Jesus called a child to Him and said, "It is not the will of my Father who is in heaven that one of these little ones should perish" (Matthew 18:14).

Why would anyone doubt that a child who dies in infancy goes straight to heaven?

Thoughtful Christians know that we have to take seriously the teaching of the Bible on original sin: "Sin came into the world through one man, and death through sin" (Romans 5:12).

All of us, born and unborn, are caught up in Adam's sin. David said, "in sin did my mother conceive me" (Psalm 51:5). This does not mean that the act leading to his conception was sinful, but that the life that was conceived was the life of a sinner from conception.

We are sinners by nature before we are sinners in practice, and it is our sinful nature that produces sinful thoughts, words, and deeds. And children who die in infancy have never heard the Gospel. They were not in a position to exercise faith. So on what basis can we believe that they enjoy the life of heaven?

We do not have a direct word of Scripture on this, but Christians through the ages have reflected on how what God has revealed in the Bible applies to this question.

The words of the Westminster Confession are helpful:

> Elect infants, dying in infancy, are regenerated, and saved by Christ through the Spirit, who worketh when, and where, and how He pleaseth: So also, are all other elect persons who are incapable of being outwardly called by the ministry of the Word.[15]

Here's what that means: The ordinary way God works is by calling people to faith and repentance through the ministry of the Word. But when it comes to infants, the unborn, or those who are "incapable of being outwardly called by the ministry of the Word," God has His own way of bringing new life to them and making them one with Christ.

God is able to regenerate them and to save them by Christ, through the Holy Spirit, and He can do this where and how and when He pleases.

A computer programmer may leave a "backdoor" by which they can gain entry into the program they have created. And in the same way, God has a "backdoor" into the hearts of infants and those who cannot comprehend His Word. Perhaps this was how John the Baptist was filled with the Holy Spirit while he was still in his mother's womb (Luke 1:15).

The Westminster Confession speaks about "elect infants," and this raises an obvious question: Are all children who die in infancy elect?

The Baptist preacher Charles Spurgeon believed that they are:

> Let every mother and father here present know assuredly that it is well with the child, if God hath taken it away from you in its infant days.

Spurgeon knew, as we have noted above, that no infant could be saved on the basis of innocence, and so he asks, "On what ground, then, do we believe the child to be saved?"

He answers:

> It is saved because it is *elect*. In the compass of election, in the Lamb's Book of Life, we believe there shall be found written millions of souls who are only shown on earth, and then stretch their wings for heaven.... If they die in infancy... they are saved.[16]

The Presbyterian theologian, Charles Hodge, believed the same. Speaking of young children, he said:

> He [Christ] evidently looked upon them as lambs of the flock for which, as the good Shepherd, He laid down His life, and of whom He said they shall never perish, and no man could pluck them out of His hands. Of such He tells us is the kingdom of heaven, as though heaven was, in great measure, composed of the souls of redeemed infants.[17]

Noting how many children die in infancy across the world, Spurgeon suggests that infant souls may constitute the great majority in heaven:

> I do not see how it is possible that so vast a number should enter heaven, unless it be on the supposition that infant souls constitute the great majority. It is a sweet belief to my own mind that there will be more saved than lost, for in all things Christ is to have the pre-eminence, and why not in this?[18]

God cares for His own, and you can be confident that a child who died in infancy, or a life that began in the womb but did not come to birth, is safe in the arms of Jesus.

One of the delights of heaven for millions who have lost a son, daughter, or sibling will be to see what that boy or girl has become and to share the joy of God's redeemed creation with them forever.

RECOMMENDED RESOURCES

ON LOSING A CHILD

Cameron Cole, *Therefore I Have Hope: 12 Truths that Comfort, Sustain and Redeem in Tragedy* (Crossway, 2018).

Cameron Cole and his wife, Lauren, suffered the sudden loss of their son, Cam, at the age of three. In his journey through grief, Cameron was sustained by twelve truths: In the initial shock: grace, gospel, resurrection, and faith. In what he describes as the "new normal:" Empathy, providence, doubt, presence, and sin. And over the long haul: Joy, service, and heaven. (200 pages).

Lianna Davis, *Made For A Different Land: Eternal Hope for Baby Loss* (Hope Mommies, 2018).

Lianna Davis and her husband, Tyler, endured the stillbirth of their daughter Noelle. Charting the course of her journey, Lianna wrestles with the theological and practical questions that confront any parent who loses a child. If God could have prevented this, why did He allow it to happen? If we are sinners by nature, how can we be sure that an infant child is in heaven? How do you navigate the enigma of being a mother when you no longer have a child to mother? How can you move forward when your heart holds on to grief and does not want to be comforted? (216 pages).

Nancy Guthrie, *Holding Onto Hope: A Pathway Through Suffering To The Heart Of God* (Tyndale, 2002).

Nancy Guthrie and her husband David suffered the loss of their daughter, Hope, who died of a metabolic disorder at around 6 months. Two years later, their son Gabriel also died of the same condition. In this compelling book, Nancy frames her story around 13 themes from the book of Job: Loss, Tears, Worship, Gratitude, Blame, Suffering, Despair, Why? Eternity, Comforters, Mystery, Submission, and Intimacy. (203 pages).

John MacArthur, *Safe in the Arms of God: Truth from Heaven About the Death of a Child* (Thomas Nelson, 2003).

Larry King asked John Macarthur, on live television, "What about a two year old baby crushed at the bottom of the World Trade Center?" "Instant heaven," Macarthur replied. This book lays out the biblical foundation for believing that children who die in infancy are in heaven. It also includes stories from people who have lost a child. (175 pages).

Mark Vroegop, *Dark Clouds, Deep Mercy: Discovering the Grace of Lament* (Crossway, 2019).

Mark Vroegop and his wife, Sarah, endured the stillbirth of their daughter Sylvia. Mark explains the importance and value of lament, which he describes as "a rich but untapped reservoir of God's grace," (p. 20). He does this first by showing us how to lament from the Psalms, and then by describing what it means to live with lament from Lamentations. He also gives a helpful guide for personal lament and for lament in the church. (223 pages).

ON SUFFERING AND LOSS

Zach Eswine, *Spurgeon's Sorrows: Realistic Hope for those who Suffer from Depression* (Christian Focus Publications, 2014).

Zack Eswine writes about depression with great insight and sensitivity. Drawing extensively from the writings of C. H. Spurgeon, Eswine describes the experience of depression, and he offers counsel on how to cope. It also includes a helpful section on how to help a person who suffers from depression. This book is full of insight, and will be of great practical help to anyone who walks the path of sorrow. (143 pages).

Nancy Guthrie, *Hearing Jesus Speak Into Your Sorrow* (Tyndale, 2009).

Writing ten years after the loss of her daughter, Hope, and then the loss of her son Gabriel, Nancy Guthrie shares the comfort and strength she found in the words of Jesus. She also writes with candor about the difficulties she faced. What does God's promise of protection mean? What about healing? Where is God in our suffering? Beautifully written and easy to read, this book feels like a conversation with a wise and compassionate friend who brings from the Bible what a grieving person most needs to hear. (165 pages).

Donald Howard, *Christians Grieve Too* (Banner of Truth, 1980).

Donald Howard's wife, Diana, contracted cancer at the age of 40. She died six years later and Howard writes, "Although through faith in Christ we were prepared for death, I was ill prepared for grief." In this short and helpful booklet, Howard explores the experience of grief, dealing especially with the issues of guilt and anger. Thoroughly biblical and written in a pastoral and accessible style, this is the best short resource of grief I have found. (30 pages).

Albert Martin, *Grieving, Hope and Solace: When a Loved One Dies in Christ* (Cruciform Press, 2011).

When Pastor Al Martin's wife, Marilyn, died, he found himself asking, "What precisely has just happened to Marilyn? What has she experienced, and what is she experiencing now?" This book offers clear answers to these questions and is especially helpful in drawing attention to what a loved one in the presence of Jesus has gained, and what still lies ahead for them, and for us, in the resurrection. (115 pages).

J. I. Packer, *A Grief Sanctified: Through Sorrow to Eternal Hope* (Crossway, 2002).

J. I. Packer introduces us to the 17th century pastor Richard Baxter, who wrote a memoir of his wife, Margaret, after she died at the age of forty-five. The memoir reflects on love, faith, death, grief, hope, and patience, and it is presented here beside J. I. Packer's own insights on grief. The 26 pages in which Packer outlines the grieving process are especially helpful. (191 pages).

ON LAMENTATIONS

Leslie C. Allen, *A Liturgy of Grief: A Pastoral Commentary on Lamentations* (Baker, 2011).

Leslie Allen is an Old Testament scholar who also serves as a hospital chaplain. In this book, he brings together insights from these two worlds, using his understanding of Lamentations to shed light on grief, and his understanding of grief to shed light on Lamentations. (195 pages).

Walter Kaiser, *Grief and Pain in the Plan of God: Christian Assurance and the Message of Lamentations* (Christian Focus Publications, 2004).

For anyone who wants to study Lamentations, this book is a great place to begin. It includes an overview of eight kinds of suffering: retributive, disciplinary, vicarious, empathetic, doxological, evidential, revelational, and eschatological, which alone is worth the price of the book! (142 pages).

Christopher Wright, *The Message of Lamentations* (Inter Varsity Press, 2015).

For those who want to explore Lamentations further, this book is a marvelous guide. It offers a faithful exposition of biblical text, helpfully applied to life in our broken world today. My copy is marked up throughout, and I warmly commend it to you. (166 pages).

ACKNOWLEDGMENTS

This book came about through the collaboration of a marvelous team of friends and colleagues, for whom I am profoundly grateful.

First among them are the dear friends who have told their stories: Lyle and Sue, Wayne and Joyce, Ken and Leslie, Stace and Kathy, and Betty and Kristen. In our conversations I felt that you were giving me a sacred trust to be shared with those who walk the path of sorrow. Thank you for your courage in choosing to help others through your testimony of faith.

Greg and Pam, whose sudden and tragic loss brought our group together, are now ministering to others who grieve, with a deep compassion that has been birthed from their own sorrow. Thank you, Greg and Pam, for your example of faithfulness in your journey through grief.

I also want to express heartfelt thanks to my friend and colleague Tim Augustyn, who made significant improvements to the manuscript; to Davis Wetherell, whose extraordinary grasp of language and eye for detail made the editing process a joy; to Gina O'Brien, who guided this project through the publication process; to Andrew Wolgemuth, whose wise counsel I greatly appreciate; to my assistant, Sandy Williams, whose help and support is an invaluable gift; and to my wife, Karen, without whom there would never have been a gathering of grieving friends in our home.

It has been a special joy to work with Jonathan Carswell, Jonathan Pountney, and all of the team at 10Publishing. The ministry of 10ofThose in selecting and supplying trusted books is a marvelous gift to the body of Christ.

And thank you, finally, to you, dear reader. My hope and prayer as you finish this book is that, by God's grace, you will be able to say:

> But this I call to mind, and therefore I have hope:
> The steadfast love of the LORD never ceases;
> his mercies never come to an end;
> they are new every morning;
> great is your faithfulness. (Lamentations 3:21-23)

ENDNOTES

1. From the hymn "It Is Well with My Soul" by Horatio G. Spafford, 1873.

2. I have adapted this description from J. I. Packer, *A Grief Sanctified* (Crossway, 2002), 9.

3. Peter Barnes, "The Loss of A Child," *Banner of Truth Magazine*, #292, 1988, 17.

4. Donald Howard, *Christians Grieve Too* (Banner of Truth, 1980), 25. Emphasis mine.

5. Eugene H. Peterson, *Five Smooth Stones for Pastoral Work* (Eerdmans, 1992), 142, 144.

6. God's people bring 17 complaints against the Lord in the first five verses of Lamentations 2. The third chapter of Lamentations follows the same pattern raising a further 19 grievances against God (Lamentations 3:2–16).

7. Peterson, *Five Smooth Stones for Pastoral Work*, 128.

8. Cited in H. Norman Wright, *Experiencing Grief* (B&H Publishing, 2004), 45–46.

9. Zack Eswine, *Spurgeon's Sorrows: Realistic Hope for Those Who Suffer from Depression* (Christian Focus Publications, 2014), 85.

10. The counselor moves between these two ministries of speaking *for* the people and speaking *to* the people throughout the book of Lamentations. Sometimes the lines are blurred, and what is said may be the shared experience of the counselor and the people together.

11. There are a few first person plural references earlier (Lamentations 4:17, 19), but these seem to be further examples of the counselor speaking for the people. Only in chapter 5 do the people finally speak for themselves.

12. C. S. Lewis, *A Grief Observed* (HarperCollins, 2001), 9.

13. Lewis, *A Grief Observed*, 52.

14. I recall this story from a sermon preached by Leith Samuel, a respected pastor and Christian leader in England, who is now with the Lord. In my office, I have a framed facsimile copy of a ticket for the *Titanic* bearing the handwritten name of J. Stuart Holden. Ken and Leslie found this during their visit to a *Titanic* exhibition in Chicago, and gave it to me. I had told the story of Harper and Holden at the funeral service for their son Kenny, and they found it helpful. The ticket is a testimony to the sovereignty of God.

15. Westminster Confessions of Faith, 10.3.

16. C. H. Spurgeon, *Infant Salvation*, Sermon #411, preached on September 29, 1861.

17. Cited in Maurice Roberts, *The Happiness of Heaven* (Reformation Heritage Books, 2009), 53.

18. Spurgeon, *Infant Salvation*.